Building a better tomorrow

RIBA PHOTOGRAPHS MONOGRAPH

Building a better tomorrow

Architecture in Britain in the 1950s

Robert Elwall

WILEY-ACADEMY

ACKNOWLEDGEMENTS

Published in collaboration with the Royal Institute of British Architects.

All illustrative material is from the British Architectural Library Photographs Collection, Royal Institute of British Architects

Front Cover: Powell & Moya / Ralph Tubbs. Skylon & Dome of Discovery, Festival of Britain, London (1951)
Photo: John Maltby

Page 2: Robert H Matthew, J Leslie Martin, Peter Moro, Edwin Williams of London County Council Architects Department. Belvedere Road entrance to the Royal Festival Hall with Trevor Dannatt's temporary canopy, South Bank, London (1951) *Photo: Colin Westwood*

Page 6: Robert H Matthew, J Leslie Martin, Peter Moro, Edwin Williams of London County Council Architects Department. Royal Festival Hall, South Bank, London (1951) *Photo: John Maltby*

First published in Great Britain in 2000 by Wiley-Academy

A division of
John Wiley & Sons
Baffins Lane
Chichester
West Sussex PO19 1UD

ISBN 0-471-98707-7

Copyright © 2000 John Wiley & Sons, Ltd and RIBA. All rights reserved. No part of this publication may be reproduced, stored in a retrieval system, or transmitted, in any form or by any means, electronic, mechanical, photocopying, recording, scanning or otherwise, except under the terms of the Copyright, Designs and Patents Act 1988 or under the terms of a licence issued by the Copyright Licensing Agency, 90 Tottenham Court Road, London, W1P 9HE, UK, without the permission in writing of the publisher.

Other Wiley Editorial Offices
New York, Weinheim, Brisbane, Singapore, Toronto

Designed and typeset by Florence Production Ltd, Stoodleigh, Devon
Printed and bound in Italy

Contents

Foreword	7
Preface	8
Introduction	9
The Festival of Britain	25
Education	30
Housing	41
Transport	69
Worship	81
Leisure and the arts	92
Commerce and industry	103
Bibliography	125
Index	126

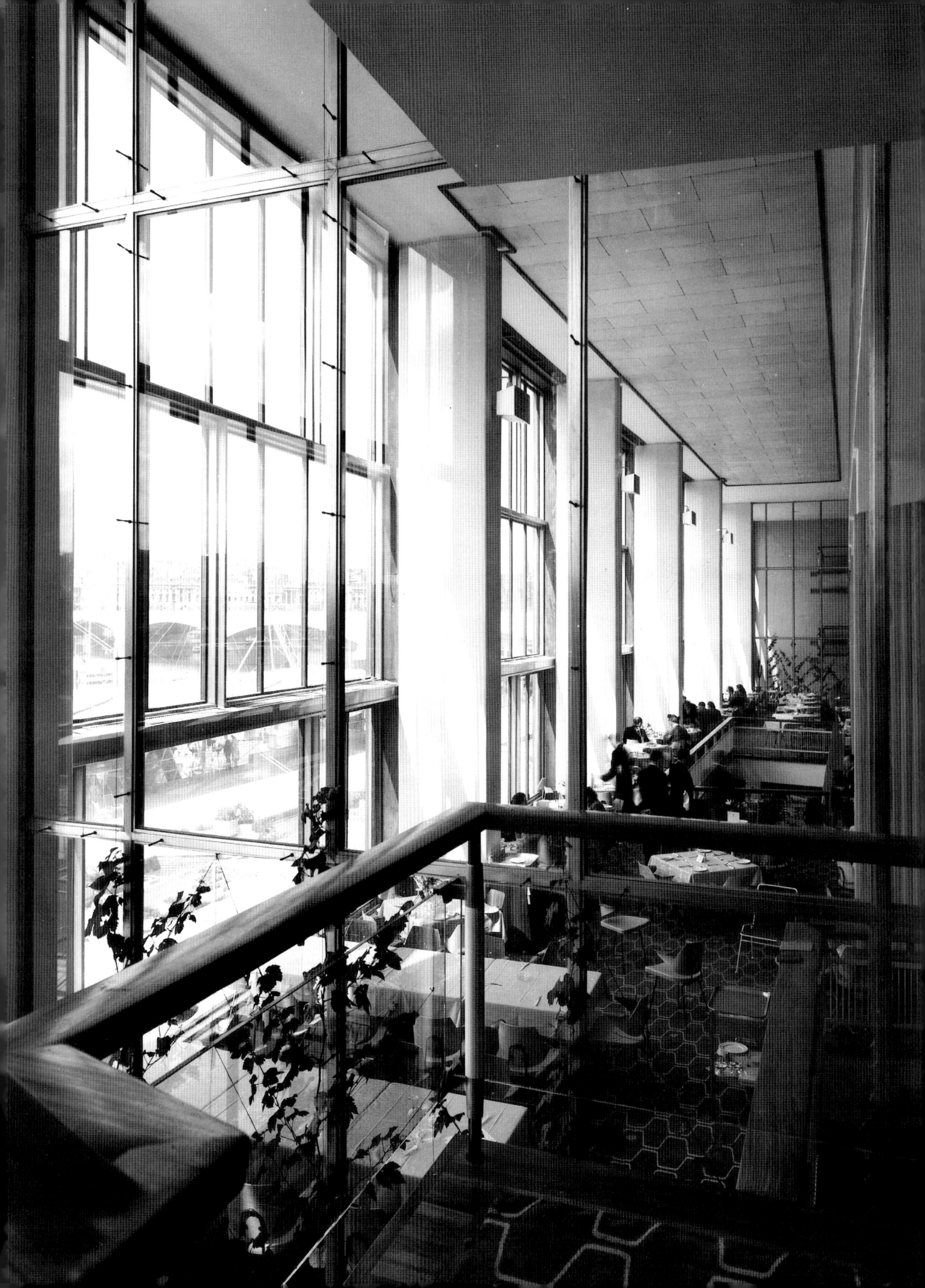

Foreword

One hundred and forty-eight years ago Queen Victoria's enthusiasm for the Great Exhibition enticed her to private views after closing time for the public. 1851 was a remarkable year and it is with photographs of that exhibition that the British Architectural Library Photographs Collection begins. The salt prints of the Great Exhibition are among its 650,000 images, collected in a wide variety of photographic formats including prints, negatives, colour transparencies, postcards and photographically illustrated books.

The RIBA started collecting this material in the 1850s and the collection is now one of the richest resources of its kind anywhere in the world. Alongside contemporary images of significant architecture from around the globe are fine examples of work by acknowledged masters of photography including Francis Bedford, Tony Ray-Jones and the architectural photographers Bedford Lemere, Dell & Wainwright and Henk Snoek. Setting aside the architectural significance of the collection, it has inestimable value as a 150-year history of photography.

The Photographs Collection is part of the British Architectural Library, the greatest collection of architectural books, drawings and manuscripts in the world. It can rightfully claim this accolade as it is unique in bringing together drawings, photographs and documentary material on architectural subjects in a single collection. Although it is regularly visited by scholars from around the world the Photographs Collection is its best-kept secret. This book will change all that.

My favourite images are of Battersea Power Station, when only half of it existed (a wonderful black-and-white photograph taken by John Maltby in 1935), and the portrait of Frank Lloyd Wright by Karsh of Ottawa from 1945 – not forgetting the marvellously utopian image by Dell & Wainwright of Ramsgate Municipal Airport (1937).

The period covered by this book, British architecture in the 1950s, is a sadly neglected subject. The young architects returning from the war brought with them a fresh and uniquely British approach to Modernism. A decade or so ago the architectural frolics of the Festival of Britain and the ensuing years were dismissed as insular and parochial. Now, with greater hindsight, we can see that the Hertfordshire schools, the housing designed by the London County Council Architects Department, the New Towns and Eric Lyons' work for the housing developers, Span, rank as world-class architecture with a uniquely British flavour. Thanks to the Photographs Collection we are all able to judge this period for ourselves.

Thankfully, the collection continues to grow; the latest acquisition includes pictures of Sir Norman Foster's transport interchange alongside the Millennium Dome on Greenwich peninsula. Gifts of material are always welcome. It is all our responsibilities to ensure that the foresight of our predecessors in the 1850s continues in our custodianship of this unique collection today.

Maxwell Hutchinson PPRIBA
April 1999

Preface

Lionel Esher's damning verdict on the 1950s – 'one of the dimmest decades in our architectural history' – has been endorsed at least tacitly by other historians and critics who, insofar as they have studied the period at all, have tended to concentrate almost exclusively on its more glamourously seductive triumphs in design. Andrew Saint's magisterial *Towards a Social Architecture: the Role of School-Building in Post-War England*, published in 1987, has been the most notable, but on the whole lonely, exception to this general trend. However, prompted in part by the transformation of the Thirties Society into the Twentieth Century Society, English Heritage's campaign to list post-war buildings, and parallels with our own era, there are signs that this attitude is beginning to change. These parallels include the expectations raised by a crushing Labour electoral victory brought about by a feeling that the time was ripe for change and renewal with the significantly entitled New Labour echoing the palingenetic tags of the 1940s and 1950s – the New Look, New Empiricism, New Brutalism, etc; the re-examination of the role of the Welfare State forged in the heady days of post-war euphoria; and the relationship between the public and private sector. In addition, the controversy surrounding the Millennium celebrations and Lord Rogers' Dome have inevitably sparked comparisons with the Festival of Britain and Ralph Tubbs' Dome of Discovery, comparisons strengthened by former 'Dome Minister' Peter Mandelson's grandfather, Herbert Morrison, having been one of the Festival's prime movers. Evidence of a heightened interest in the 1950s can now be seen in aspects as diverse as television comedy and drama, the rise of tower block chic, the Imperial War Museum's nostalgic exhibition *From the Bomb to the Beatles* or the recent enlightening exhibition and book devoted to the work of Tayler & Green.

Although this is a book nominally on the 1950s, decades are, of course, artificial constructs which are constantly undermined by historical developments and therefore a small number of buildings which throw light on the period have been included even though they fall outside its strict confines. It is also a book of black-and-white archival photographs drawn almost entirely from the RIBA's collection. While this cannot do justice to the imaginative use of colour made by architects of the period, it does reflect the way architecture was most commonly seen through reproduction. With the most obvious exception of some of Michael Wickham's photographs for *House and Garden*, black-and-white continued to be the photographer's chosen medium and it is part of the aim of this book to pay tribute to the skill of 1950s' architectural practitioners such as John Maltby, John Pantlin, Colin Westwood and John McCann. Within these confines the book seeks to give a general introductory overview of the period and to suggest that despite Esher's censure it would repay further, more detailed, study. The themes of the 1950s – the social responsibility of the architect; the architect's relationship to other design and building professionals; where and how we should build – remain as relevant and challenging today as they were then.

I have benefited enormously from the help and advice of a great number of people and would like to thank: Kaye Bagshaw, Dr Neil Bingham, Sally Dale, Renata Gross, Bob Maguire, David and Mary Medd; Lucy Archer, Bill Godfrey of James Cubitt & Partners, Leslie Gooday, Patrick Gwynne, Alice Moro and Pat Campeau, all of whom have either generously donated photographs to the collection or have made available images from their private archives to fill gaps in ours; Andrew Mead of the *Architects' Journal* for the supply of images of Bracken House and St Paul's, Bow Common; Maggie Toy and Mariangela Palazzi-Williams of Wiley-Academy, a fitting publisher as it was during the 1950s that *Architectural Design* first emerged with a truly distinctive voice; A C Cooper, particularly Lorraine Finch-Hawkes, for the copy photography and printing. My biggest debt, however, is to my wife Cathy whose organizational powers and unstinting help should not go unsung.

Introduction

The 1950s was a decade of contrast, paradox and variety. It began with prefabs, utility furniture and building restrictions and ended with a growing number of high-rise blocks, television sets and a building boom. In 1950 professionals like C H Aslin and Frederick Gibberd were key players on the architectural stage; by 1959 the spotlight had shifted to property developers such as Jack Cotton and Lew Hammerson. As the era of post-war austerity gave way to increased affluence, famously signalled by Harold Macmillan's rousing declaration that 'most of our people have never had it so good', a brilliant, but all too brief, flowering of public sector architecture bowed to a sharp resurgence of private practice. It was a decade when reconstruction afforded the architect unparalleled opportunities but when a more planned and technocratic approach to design, which emphasized the environment and the programme rather than the individual monument, threatened his status and autonomy. Further, it was a time when influences from a more prosperous abroad vied with a heightened interest and pride in 'the Englishness of English art' and an indigenous 'functional tradition'; when Modernism, marginalized in the 1930s, became the official architecture of the Welfare State, but when, in its very moment of triumph, the debate about its nature and form had never been more intense.

Far from being a decade of crabbed uniformity, as some critics have posited, the 1950s was marked by stylistic diversity. Encompassing works as differing as the Hertfordshire schools, Tayler & Green's rural housing and Stirling & Gowan's flats at Ham Common, Modernism itself was far from monolithic, nor, despite what the modernist filters of the *Architectural Review* and the *Architects' Journal* encouraged their readers to believe, had Modernism expunged other forms of architectural creativity. A robust classical tradition persisted while a clutch of ecclesiastical architects demonstrated their continuing facility in the Gothic manner. In addition, for many people the reality of their architectural experience was limited to the spec builders' historical pastiche.

The *Architect & Building News* greeted the new decade with an editorial which reflected the prevailing melancholy mood: 'If the post-war years can teach us anything at all it is that false optimism leads to disappointment . . . The actual number of bricks laid may be a source of satisfaction to those who really know just how many we can afford today. But there are singularly few signs that architects have anything fresh to say.'[1] Despite this lament, however, much had been achieved since 1945 when Labour's electoral victory marked a national determination to create a post-war social order which would be humane, equitable, planned and, above all, new – the Welfare State allied to a modernist architecture would help to ensure there would be no return to the grim, depression days of the 1930s.

Alongside that for social provision, the legislative framework for reconstruction had been put in place by a series of Acts, the most important of which were the New Towns Act (1946) and the Town and Country Planning Act (1947). Under the provisions of the former 14 New Towns had been initiated by 1950 in an attempt to relieve urban congestion through central planning rather than unchecked suburban sprawl. The latter Act revolutionized land-use control by making virtually all new development subject to permission by a greatly reduced number of planning authorities whose decisions were to be informed by the overall development plans they were required to formulate. In housing, where the need was most

Coronation decorations, London (1953)
Photo: John McCann

urgent, many damaged homes had been repaired and new ones erected, initially through the provision of supposedly temporary prefabs and then, from 1946, by the institution of an ambitious programme of new, permanent public housing. Here, following the proposals of Patrick Abercrombie and J H Forshaw's *County of London Plan* (1943), London boroughs such as Finsbury and Hackney led the way. In school building, the first batch of Hertfordshire schools was just being finished in 1950 while the completion of Sir Giles Gilbert Scott's reconstruction of the House of Commons symbolized the survival of democratic values. Even so, the beginning of the new decade was characterized by frustration and disillusionment. The war had provided an opportunity to take stock and its end saw a release of pent-up energy with demobbed young architects eager to translate the lessons of their wartime experience and modernist aspirations into peacetime practice. Confronted by the harsh realities of materials shortages, building licences, an economic downturn and a worsening foreign situation, this euphoria evaporated. Consequently some architects such as Maxwell Fry and Jane Drew, Raglan Squire (prosecuted for exceeding the terms of a building licence) and James Cubitt decided their salvation lay in practice overseas.

It was against this gloomy backdrop of faltering recovery that the Festival of Britain (1951) was conceived as 'a tonic to the nation'.[2] To most architects the gentle, Swedish-inspired Modernism of the

**Chamberlin Powell & Bon.
Golden Lane Estate, City of
London, London (1957)**
Photo: John Maltby

pavilions represented nothing new, and James Holland, controller of display in the upstream area, later expressed the feelings of many when he maintained that 'Far from initiating a period and a style, I believe that the Festival summarized an epoch, it was an ending rather than a beginning'.[3] To the public, however, it was a revelation. Light, airy, informal and scaled to people, the Festival site seemed less a remembrance of things past, more an intimation of a brighter, modernist future to come.

As the publicly acceptable face of Modernism the 'Festival style' spread rapidly, influencing shop and exhibition design, the 1953 Coronation, lighting, lettering, interior decoration and a host of manufactured goods. Festival-inspired details abounded on housing estates and in airports, pubs and coffee bars in a process of 'Contemporary' debasement which the Festival's organizers deplored. Besides the Royal Festival Hall, the Festival's most significant and enduring legacy, however, lay in the lessons its irregular layout afforded for urban planning. Its main landscape characteristics, which were described by the *Architectural Review* as 'expectation and suspense, the relaxation provided by the quiet enclosure, the shock of the surprising view, the contrast of the familiar with the unexpected, changes of level, tempo and scale',[4] exercised a profound influence on the planning of New Towns such as Stevenage and the redevelopment of many city centres, as well as on the layout of housing estates and, in the next decade, university campuses.

The Festival's approach to landscape was rightly regarded by the art critic, Lawrence Alloway, as 'the crown of the British picturesque revival'.[5] This revival had gathered momentum in the early 1940s with a series of articles in the *Architectural Review* by Nikolaus Pevsner, Susan Lang and the garden historian, H F Clark, and evolved into the concept of 'Townscape' which was articulated through the seductive drawings of Gordon Cullen and to which the December 1949 issue of the *Architectural Review* was largely devoted. The attempt to relate picturesque theories to contemporary practice and the notion of townscape remained important themes throughout the 1950s being further emphasized by Pevsner's Reith Lectures of 1955, which were published in the following year as *The Englishness of English Art*, and culminating in his portrayal of the London County Council's modernist housing at Roehampton as 'eminently English' and in the eighteenth-century landscape tradition.[6] Underlying these writings was a conscious attempt to establish an anglicized form of the International Style with its own native ancestry and thereby refute the widely held pre-war view that Modernism was essentially a foreign import imposed by a handful of émigrés on an English scene of which they had little understanding. In this respect the iconography of the Festival in celebrating Britain's land and people in a modernist setting was highly significant. In both its built environment and fundamental principles, therefore, the Festival set the architectural agenda for much of the decade which architects could either choose to follow or rebel against.

Opportunities for the private architect during the early 1950s were severely limited by a system of building licences which channelled scarce materials and resources into the priority areas of housing and schools. Born, in Labour's case, of a concern to eradicate social injustice, but also of a general recognition that the vast programme of reconstruction could not be tackled by the piecemeal efforts of the private sector, these were both fields for which the government had assumed greater responsibility. Consequently these years were dominated by public authority architecture either designed directly or commissioned by central government departments; by county councils (responsible for school building); by city, borough and district councils (responsible for housing); and by the New Town Development Corporations financed by the Ministry of Town and Country Planning. Though to greatly varying degrees, such bodies alone possessed the resources and could allow the continuity necessary to carry out major building programmes and the research and development which underpinned them. The result was that by 1955 nearly half the country's architects were employed in public offices while many of the remainder subsisted on a diet of work farmed out to them by authorities which were overstretched.

This dramatic shift from the private to the public sector represented a radical change in the pattern of architectural practice and caused friction in a profession which clung tenaciously to the ideal of the architect as an independent creator and still regarded official architecture, despite its distinguished pedigree, with the disdain evident in President of the RIBA Goodhart-Rendel's dismissal of it as 'stale chocolate'.[7] While it is true that much second-rate architecture, stigmatized by critics as 'make do and mend', emerged from these public bodies, many of which developed unwieldy bureaucracies, their achievement must be placed in the context of the parlous economic circumstances which often forced reductions in space and amenities or the use of lower grade materials. Good work, however, is not hard to find whether it be the schools built in Middlesex under the direction of the County Architect, C G Stillman; the enlightened initiatives undertaken by Donald Gibson, firstly as City Architect of Coventry and then as County Architect of Nottinghamshire; or housing schemes such as Chamberlin Powell & Bon's Golden Lane Estate, London (1957), or those executed by Tayler & Green for Loddon Rural District Council. Doubtless many architects entered public offices because these were the only source of employment, but we should not underestimate the pervasive idealism of the post-war years which motivated architects to believe that they should look beyond the mere reshaping of the physical fabric to the creation of a more just society. It was in the Hertfordshire school building programme and the housing designed by the London County Council, both of which were immensely influential and set new standards of public authority architecture, where the concept of architecture as a social service was most potently expressed.

Hertfordshire County Architects Department. Little Green Lanes Junior School, Croxley Green (1949)

The Hertfordshire programme of 'light and dry', steel-framed schools, which owed much to Walter Gropius' ideas on prefabrication and the pre-war nursery school movement, also drew on the wartime experience of operational research gained by two of its authors, Stirrat Johnson-Marshall and David Medd, who were colleagues at the Camouflage Development and Training Centre in Surrey. Medd recalled their role there as 'part of a chain in a complete cycle which didn't repeat but evolved as it went round: policy, thinking, designing, making, using, new policy, rethinking and so on. The designer was a link in a complete chain'.[8] Here was the essence of Hertfordshire's collaborative approach which bore fruit in a series of progressive, child-centred schools which in their Meccano-like structures greatly influenced later architects such as Cedric Price, Richard Rogers and Norman Foster. The *Architects' Journal* summed up Hertfordshire's achievement thus:

> School design could under the guise of 'modern architecture', and littered with smart clichés, have extolled the values of State education, or the authority and power of the teacher, or the artistic outpourings of some architectural soul bent on self-aggrandisement. Instead, the best of our post-war schools set a pattern, a rhythm of behaviour, for the child, in three dimensions, which emphasizes what he should do, and with colour, form, light and space, exercises his power of imagination and appreciation.[9]

The Hertfordshire credo was spread to the Ministry of Education and other authorities not just by the county's willingness to share its research and fund of accumulated experience but also by the extraordinary number of its former employees who filled key posts elsewhere. In 1950 a group of architects including A W Cleeve Barr and Oliver Cox left Hertfordshire to join the newly reformed Housing Division of the London County Council. The extent of its programme and the size of its individual jobs, which were large enough to reach into the realms of planning, presented the ultimate challenge to such socially conscious architects. After 1945 the scale and urgency of the need to replenish its housing stock had seen the council transfer

INTRODUCTION 13

Tayler & Green. Church Road, Bergh Apton (1957)

responsibility for housing from its architects' department to that of the valuer, a move, not surprisingly, condemned by the architectural press which criticized the 'unimaginative layouts, the poor design and the crude detailing'[10] of the work produced. After a sustained campaign, a new Housing Division was set up in 1950 headed by H J Whitfield Lewis who reported to the LCC's chief architect, Robert Matthew, and his deputy, Leslie Martin. Matthew reorganized the department dividing it on functional rather than regional lines and replacing its bureaucratic, pyramidal structure with a group pattern which fostered team working and devolved responsibility. This reorganization, together with the warm critical reception given to the Royal Festival Hall, saw the LCC go from strength to strength. By 1956 it employed a staff of over three thousand, with the ranks of its largest division, housing, having swollen from a staff of 20 in 1950 to over four hundred, and boasted resources and power other authorities could only envy. This was the platform for a programme of ground-breaking social housing guided by the strategy outlined in the council's Development Plan of 1951 which incorporated many of the recommendations made previously by Abercrombie and Forshaw. Culminating during the 1950s in Alton West Estate at Roehampton (1959), this programme earned critical plaudits at home and abroad, was generally popular with the tenants, and was regarded as an exemplar by other authorities, not least in its embracing of mixed development and progressively taller blocks.

In their attempts to forge an architecture suited to the requirements of the nascent Welfare State it is not surprising that architects should have looked to Sweden, with its state provision of low-cost housing and wide-ranging welfare facilities, as a role model. For the generation of architects trained before the war, the lure of Sweden was already strong, *suedoiserie* having been a potent force in the 1930s particularly in the wake of Gunnar Asplund's designs for the *Exhibition of Modern Industrial and Decorative Arts*, Stockholm (1930). Neutral during the war, Sweden had enjoyed uninterrupted building activity, but by 1947 the *Architectural Review* was drawing attention to a change in direction in its architecture and extolling its merits to its readers. The chief characteristic of the change, which the *Architectural Review* labelled 'The New Empiricism', was a reaction against the overly rigid formalism of the International Style expressed in a 'workaday common sense', experimental and undogmatic spirit. Its main elements were freer planning and fenestration; a readiness to use traditional materials where

BUILDING A BETTER TOMORROW

appropriate; a sensitivity to site and landscape; a return to 'cosiness' in domestic architecture; and a recognition of the importance of psychology in design.[11] Denoting a more flexible approach to Modernism, the New Empiricism therefore paralleled the *Architectural Review*'s simultaneous promotion of picturesque informality while also reflecting the similar development of a more practical vernacular modernist aesthetic which some British architects had begun to pursue before war intervened. Perceived as being a more humane form of Modernism and accordingly also dubbed 'The New Humanism', the Swedish spirit infected the Herts architects and their colleagues at the LCC. Mary Crowley, whose understanding of children's educational and psychological requirements and how these could be satisfied architecturally was the bedrock of Hertfordshire's success, had worked in social service in Scandinavia, and Guy Oddie, himself a Herts architect, significantly entitled his article looking back at post-war school building, 'The New English Humanism'.[12] At the LCC, Alton East Estate (1955) represented the apogee of Swedish influence on its Housing Division while the Swedish motifs clearly discernible at the Royal Festival Hall and the Festival of Britain generally helped to give them wide currency.

Scandinavian influence was also apparent in the largest public building enterprise of the period, the New Towns. By providing a *tabula rasa* for planners and architects and throwing into sharp relief some of the key issues of the day – flats versus houses; high- versus low-density; optimum use of land – the New Towns aroused great expectations and equally great criticism. Intended to counteract urban sprawl and help address the housing problem, the 1946 New Towns Act combined the ideals of the Garden City Movement, tirelessly promulgated by Frederic Osborn and the Town and Country Planning Association with, disappointingly from their point of view, central government funding and the state provision of housing. Also underlying the Act was Abercrombie's *Greater London Plan* (1944) which had advocated the dispersal of population to a series of New Towns sited beyond the green belt. This represented a policy of planned decentralization and satellite development which, though predicated on what later proved to be a false assumption of a country changing only slowly, provided a model for other urban areas throughout the 1950s.

Although the sites differed, as Abercrombie had recommended, eight of the first 14 New Towns were intended to deal with London overspill, the others being Aycliffe, Peterlee, Cwmbran, Corby, East Kilbride and Glenrothes. These Mark I New Towns were to be self-contained and cater for populations of around fifty thousand. Nearly all embraced the principle of the neighbourhood unit, borrowed from American planning, which characteristically provided clusters of five to ten thousand people with a primary school, shops and other facilities in an attempt to foster community spirit. Most New Town housing was to its residents reassuringly conventional and marked by a low ratio of flats, a preponderance of two-storey terraced houses with gardens, the use of traditional materials like brick and little prefabrication. Although Frederick Gibberd, chief architect of the best designed New Town, Harlow, maintained that 'the English School of Landscape design (probably the country's greatest contribution to art) has been revived and given a new dimension largely by the New Town Movement',[13] the towns soon came under attack, most witheringly in a 1953 article by Jim Richards where he berated their lack of infrastructure which rendered them no more than isolated groups of housing estates; their cumbersome bureaucracy and inadequate financing; but most of all their lack of urban qualities – 'They consist for the most part of scattered two-storey dwellings, separated by great spaces. Their inhabitants, instead of feeling themselves secure within an environment devoted to their convenience and pleasure, find themselves marooned in a desert of grass verges and concrete roadways.'[14] Richards' conclusion that the Englishman 'today goes on building suburbs which he dignifies by the name of towns' was supported by Cullen's photographs and drawings carefully composed to indict what Cullen termed the New Towns' 'prairie planning'.[15] Although Hugh Wilson's proposed layout for Cumbernauld, the only additional New Town designated during the decade (in 1956), sought to redress these problems by aiming for higher densities in a more compact plan, by the end of the 1950s the New Towns had proved only a limited success. The towns' visual uniformity had spurred the arguments for mixed development; the neighbourhood unit had been undermined by increased mobility; and the towns' failure to provide the hoped for definitive solution to

Chamberlin Powell & Bon. Bousfield Primary School, South Kensington, London (1956)
Photo: John Maltby

the problem of overspill, now exacerbated by unforeseen population growth and movement, saw a reversion in the 1960s to high-density, inner-city redevelopment with disastrous consequences. The New Town story was one of honest endeavour but unrealistically high expectations which resulted in disappointment.

Public architecture thrived not merely because of the sheer extent of rebuilding but also because of its increased technical complexity. Research and development were terms frequently cited in these years and were evidence of the desire to harness science and technology, crucial to the war effort, to the fulfilment of peacetime social aspirations. The 'boffins' war' was to be transformed into the benevolent, technologically informed architects' peace. Testifying to the more scientific strain in architectural practice, which, with its emphasis on rational analysis of the problem prior to design, was one of the concerns of the Modern Movement, were several factors. Notable among them were the influential, educative activities of the RIBA's Architectural Science Group founded in 1941; the increased prevalence of development groups – following the success of that set up by Stirrat Johnson-Marshall at the Ministry of Education, nine government departments had established similar groups by 1961; and the formation of the Modular Society in 1953 by Mark Hartland Thomas to promote dimensional coordination. Of most importance, however, was the Building Research Station (BRS), the role of which had been greatly enlarged during the war and which employed for a time architects such as Cecil Handisyde, John Eastwick-Field and Donald Gibson who were to play significant parts in shaping post-war architecture. With its testing of building materials and methods, the BRS provided architects with a steady flow of essential information. The Hertfordshire architects, for example, relied heavily on advice from the BRS, conveniently situated within the county's borders at Garston, particularly from its Architectural Physics Division which investigated matters of environmental science. This division also played a key role in the acoustical design of the Royal Festival Hall, a building which exemplified the new technological approach to architecture.

Prefabrication was also a sign of the growing hold of technology on building. Adopted initially as an emergency measure after the war to speed up building of the required number of houses and schools, prefabrication came to be viewed by some architects, manufacturers and government ministries as a key instrument of Welfare State policy. A new era required a new, simpler method of building which, declared Stirrat Johnson-Marshall, one of prefabrication's staunchest advocates, 'must combine the skills of the architect, the Building Research Station, the builder and the manufacturer, in a team in which each member can make his contribution at the inception of a project and not at different stages in the process of building'.[16] Not only would prefabrication reduce dirty and dangerous sitework and overcome labour shortages, it would transform society through the mass production of cheap buildings with limited life spans. Despite the impetus given to industrialized building by the Herts schools and professional recognition of its importance symbolized by C H Aslin's elevation to the RIBA presidency in 1954, these technocratic dreams remained unfulfilled. The very success of the Hertfordshire programme encouraged the proliferation of other systems and, with little progress in modular coordination, each developed its own set of unique components. In housing, the LCC's various experiments with prefabricated systems such as that at Picton Street, Camberwell (1955), proved disappointing. In addition, increased prosperity and rising expectations in the latter part of the decade occasioned a change in public attitudes to prefabrication, which came to be regarded as an outworn temporary palliative of the detested Cripps era. Above all, there was little proof that prefabrication could actually deliver its promised cost benefits, and, as building materials became readily available once again, traditional building revived. By the mid-1950s, highlighted by the traditionally built, elegant and economic example of Powell & Moya's Mayfield School, Putney (1955), only a quarter of new schools were being constructed by non-traditional methods. However, many of the techniques used in prefabrication together with factory-made components helped to revitalize and rationalize traditional building.

The technical complexities of building also encouraged the emergence of large private firms incorporating a wide range of expertise such as Yorke Rosenberg & Mardall, and multidisciplinary working of the kind seen in practices like Architects' Co-Partnership and Farmer & Dark where the engineer was regarded as an essential member of the design team. Indeed, the confluence of architecture and engineering was a significant feature of the 1950s, and was personified in the career of Ove Arup, who was instrumental in the development of reinforced concrete cross-wall construction – arguably the most important structural innovation of the period – and 'without whose collaboration', asserted the historian Henry-Russell Hitchcock, 'no notable work seems even to proceed'.[17] This greater involvement of the engineer was one of a number of factors conspiring to undermine the role of the architect as traditionally perceived. These included the rise of the public architect with enlarged social responsibilities which reached beyond those to his immediate client, and the growth in team working which required subordination of the individual personality to the collective effort – 'I don't want any prima donnas or little Corbs'[18] announced W D Pile at the Ministry of Education. Moreover, there was a shift in emphasis away from the discrete work to the building conceived as part of a wider programme often involving other competing professionals, especially planners, while the perils of prefabrication threatened to reduce the role of the architect to a mere assembler of kit parts. All these vindicated John Summerson's judgement that the architect 'stands in a challenged, critical position'.[19]

The debate about the architect's role and, more crucially, the future direction architecture should take intensified with the abolition of building licences in November 1954 and the subsequent revival of private practice which precipitated an exodus from public office of core personnel such as Stirrat Johnson-Marshall and Chief Architect to the LCC, Leslie Martin. 'And Then There Were . . .' lamented the *Architects' Journal* in a poignant editorial in 1956[20] which correctly sensed that, though its workload was continuing to increase, the halcyon days of public architecture were drawing to a close. Despite the social commitment of private architects such as Walter Segal or Architects' Co-Partnership, a new era of private capital investment, which meant architects were no longer restricted to a narrow range of essential building types, would place a higher premium on personal expression than on social idealism.

By 1954 although pre-war traditionalists like Giles Gilbert Scott and Goodhart-Rendel remained active, the careers of most of their 1930s modernist counterparts had petered out. Berthold Lubetkin, whose research-based Modernism should have found fertile soil after 1945, completed a few housing schemes, most of which had been conceived before the war, became Architect-Planner to Peterlee New Town in 1948 and then resigned, disillusioned, two years later. Henceforth he was to be a peripheral figure. After a fleeting appearance designing the Telekinema at the Festival of Britain, Wells Coates' career similarly expired, while Maxwell Fry was mainly engaged abroad, principally in Nigeria and Chandigarh. With Amyas Connell practising in East Africa and Basil Ward combining teaching with a largely conventional architectural practice, Colin Lucas, alone, of the partnership whose uncompromisingly modern designs of the 1930s were much admired by the 1950s young Turks, was left to fulfil his ideals by becoming one of the leading lights of the LCC's Housing Division which he joined in 1950. Of those who could boast a significant body of pre-war work, only F R S Yorke (joined in 1944 by the Czech émigré, Eugene Rosenberg, and the Finn, Cyril Mardall) and Ernö Goldfinger continued to flourish in the 1950s. The mantle had passed to a new generation of modernists, chief among their numbers in private practice being Hugh Casson, orchestrator not just of the Festival of Britain but of the Coronation decorations too; Frederick Gibberd, who besides being chief architect at Harlow New Town, obtained a string of prestigious commissions; and Basil Spence, whose victory in the Coventry Cathedral competition of 1951 relaunched a career which had threatened to see him typecast as an exhibition designer after his successful contributions to the *Britain Can Make It* exhibition (1946) and the Festival of Britain. Together with critics and historians such as Jim Richards and Nikolaus Pevsner, both of whom were on the *Architectural Review*'s editorial board, these architects constituted the backbone of the new modernist establishment – a status confirmed when Spence became President of the RIBA in 1958. The fact that all were in their forties underlined the results of a 1953 survey which showed that three-quarters of all firms' principals were at least that age.

This generation came under attack from a still younger generation including Alison and Peter Smithson, Colin St John Wilson and James Stirling, all of whom had trained during or just after the war and felt excluded by their elders from the most important jobs. To these younger architects the whimsical populism of the Festival of Britain, the loose 'octopus' planning of the Hertfordshire schools, the 'sharawaggi' of the picturesque revival and the indulgent romanticism of 'Scando' were a betrayal of the Modern Movement, a deviation from the true path mapped out by the revered masters of its 'heroic' age and English primitives like Connell Ward & Lucas. Just as modern had been diluted into fashionable 'moderne' by architects like Oliver Hill in the 1930s, so now it had spawned a bastard offspring, 'Contemporary', infected with those worst of English vices, compromise and sentimentality. The reaction to this popularization of Modernism and its degeneration into a mere style was a 'retreat to order'[21] which resulted in a tougher, more rigorous architecture as noted by Lionel Brett, 'It was inevitable . . . that there would be a reaction from the rather feminine elegance of the South Bank Exhibition, with its light floating roofs, its doves and wires and lacy white balustrades and its expurgated Victoriana. All that has gone with the New Look, and in its place we have chunky masonry, heavy lintels, black painted tubular balustrades, and the brutal exposure of naked materials and services.'[22]

The first manifestation of this reaction was the Smithsons' Hunstanton School (1954) which betrayed the influence of Mies van der Rohe, whose American work had been made known in England by the publication of Philip Johnson's 1948 monograph, and of Professor Rudolf Wittkower's seminal *Architectural Principles in the Age of Humanism* (1949). This latter, together with the teachings and writings of Wittkower's pupil, Colin Rowe, served to re-emphasize the classical basis of Modernism reckoned by Reyner Banham to lie in 'its abstract intellectual disciplines (proportion,

Patrick Gwynne. The Firs, Hampstead, London (1959)

symmetry) and habits of mind (clarity, rationalism) far more than matters of detailed style'.[23] The significance of Hunstanton as an emphatic rejection of the principles underlying the Hertfordshire programme was immediately apparent to contemporaries and provoked a commensurably vitriolic response, the *Architects' Journal*'s editor, Colin Boyne, condemning it as 'a formalist structure which will please only the architects, and a small coterie concerned more with satisfying their personal design sense than with achieving a humanist, functional architecture'.[24]

Although the Smithsons built little in the decade after Hunstanton they remained influential through their polemical writings; exhibition displays such as that for *This is Tomorrow* and the *House of the Future* (both 1956); and their unsuccessful competition entries for Coventry Cathedral (1951) and Golden Lane (1952). Heavily influenced by the sociological research into East End life of Judith Henderson and the photographs of her husband, Nigel, the Golden Lane entry posited a kinetic form of urbanism and introduced the idea of a 'streets-in-the-air' solution to mass housing. Presented to the ninth Congrès Internationaux d'Architecture Moderne (CIAM) at Aix-en-Provence in 1953, the scheme based on 'patterns of association' presented a direct challenge to the Athens Charter of 1933 with its separation of the city into zoned areas. The generational conflict that ensued and the establishment of Team X, with the Smithsons among its leading protagonists, resulted in CIAM's eventual demise and that of its English arm, the MARS Group, in 1957.

The tougher attitude to architectural design revealed in the Smithsons' work was paralleled by the rise of a new breed of hard-nosed critics. These included Banham and Ian Nairn, both of whom were members of the *Architectural Review*'s editorial staff, and Theo Crosby, from 1953 technical editor of *Architectural Design*, a magazine which was coming to supplant the increasingly equivocal *Architectural Review* as the mouthpiece of the avant-garde. It was Banham, a member with the Smithsons of the Independent Group, who developed and popularized the term 'New Brutalism' to describe the fresh mood. According to Banham its main attributes, buttressed by a ruthless logic, were memorability of the building as image, the clear

Sir Albert Richardson. Bracken House, Cannon Street, London (1959) *Photo: Alan Williams*

exhibition of structure, and the valuation of materials for their inherent qualities 'as found'. 'In the last resort what characterizes the New Brutalism in architecture', Banham declared, 'is precisely its brutality, its *je m'en foutisme*, its bloody-mindedness.'[25] Related to the *art brut* of Jean Dubuffet, New Brutalism took its architectural inspiration initially not just from Wittkower but from the monumental Baroque designs of Vanbrugh and Hawksmoor before its emphasis shifted towards the *béton brut* work of Le Corbusier, notably the Unité d'Habitation, Marseilles (1952), and the Maisons Jaoul, Paris (1956). Along with Le Corbusier's *Le Modulor* (1950), these works greatly influenced a whole generation of British architects before Le Corbusier fell into disrepute in the late 1960s.

Works admitted to the New Brutalist canon by Banham included the six houses at South Hill Park, London (1956), by Stanley Amis and Bill and Gillian Howell, Lyons Israel & Ellis' Old Vic Annexe, London (1958), and the LCC's Alton West Estate which represented a victory for the 'hardline Corbusians' over the 'soft Swedes' in a fierce struggle to define Modernism. Likening them to 'an encounter with some Kline paintings or Hecht-Hill-Lancaster films – a smart blow on the head with a carefully shaped blunt instrument',[26] Banham's attempt to claim Stirling & Gowan's flats at Ham Common, London (1958), as a key work of New Brutalism was angrily repudiated by the architects, who reckoned the term was too narrow and had 'created in the public eye an image of pretentiousness, artiness and irresponsibility . . . the continuation of its use can only be detrimental to modern architecture in this country'.[27] Despite its Corbusian references, Ham Common drew on a variety of influences, in particular the contemporaneous studies by Jim Richards, with Eric de Maré's evocative photographs, of the 'functional tradition' of Britain's early industrial buildings. It was thus indicative of a much more broadly based reaction, of which New Brutalism was only the most extreme, but nevertheless influential, manifestation, to what many architects regarded as the selling short of Modernism.

Far removed from the strident sublimity and non-specificity to place of the New Brutalist ethic, yet still quintessentially modern, was the quiet, self-effacing rural housing, respectful of local traditions, of Tayler & Green. In 1957 Tayler summed up the partnership's design philosophy thus:

> True simplicity is entirely lacking in English modern architecture. Instead there is an attempt at cerebral sophistication too glossy and smarty, quite unsuited to the English . . . The end should be this: an appropriate, functional, varied, realistic character within the modern style. A democratic architecture; this would be something new for this country. It is what Modern is not; it entirely lacks a vernacular, a style easy enough to imitate well universally. Any style can be imitated badly, which is what happens with the style called 'Contemporary.' On the other hand, a formalistic architecture is always attractive to architects and always inconvenient to their clients. Classical architecture, superb in the right place, chills in the wrong one.[28]

Tayler & Green's housing, paralleled in an urban setting by that of Eric Lyons and Span, demonstrated that Modernism could incorporate picturesque elements without lapsing into sentimental Romanticism, could be sensitive to the *genius loci* and could thereby create a genuinely popular environment.

These contrasting attitudes betokened a greater variety in architectural design. While firms such as Chamberlin Powell & Bon and Yorke Rosenberg & Mardall refused to swap the constrictions of austerity for the straitjacket of New Brutalism they nevertheless conceived works of an increasingly forceful character. In the former's case the Japanese-style refinement of Bousfield Primary School, London (1956), judged by the American critic, George Kidder Smith, to be 'one of the best schools in Europe'[29] gave way to the Jaoul-inspired forms of Crescent House, Golden Lane Estate (1958–62). In the latter's case the injection of new, younger blood, exemplified by such architects as David Allford, saw the firm not untypically embrace a more rigorously analytical approach to design. These firms were also part of a trend towards the establishment of larger practices such as Powell & Moya, Robert Matthew & Johnson-Marshall and Gollins Melvin Ward & Partners which adopted working procedures derived from the public sector and which were to be dominant forces in British architecture in the ensuing decades.

Pursuing a more independent line were mavericks like Ernö Goldfinger and Denys Lasdun who largely distanced themselves from the decade's more fractious polemics. The tougher architectural climate suited Goldfinger's evolution of a highly personal style based on the reduction of designs to their basic elements: 'big decks – platforms one on top of the other';[30] adherence to the discipline of a 2 ft 9 in grid to streamline production and aid standardization of details; and the use of a strictly limited range of materials. Lasdun's work by contrast was more expressive, rejecting the mechanistic formalism of much contemporary architecture and in Hallfield School, Paddington, London (1955), and the cluster housing blocks at Usk Street (1955) and Claredale Street (1959), both in London's Bethnal Green, gradually articulating an architectural language which was to be most eloquently stated in the 1960s. For smaller firms like these, however, it was the private house, though often subject to bureaucratic planning controls, which afforded the best opportunity for creative expression. Among those not featured may be mentioned Trevor Dannatt's house in Clarkson Road, Cambridge (1959), with its Scandinavian-like use of timber; Patrick Gwynne's curvaceous and typically elegant The Firs, Hampstead, London (1959), distinguished by its employment of varied materials and fitments designed by the architect; and houses by Morris & Steedman such as Avisfield, Edinburgh (1957), which sought to establish a modern form of Scottish domestic architecture by blending a mixture of sources both American and Japanese. Perhaps the most imaginative domestic architect of the period, however, was Peter Womersley to whose Farnley Hey, Farnley Tyas (1955), could be added his house for the textile designer, Bernat Klein, at High Sunderland (1957).

As the battle for the soul of Modernism raged, a small minority of architects, largely ignored by the professional press, swam against the tide by continuing to give creative expression to traditional styles. This was most evident in country house architecture where a surprisingly large number of new houses were built often replacing older ones which had been sold or demolished. Most of these were neo-Georgian and executed by architects such as Claud Phillimore, who established a flourishing practice, or the more talented Yorkshire-based Francis Johnson. That other bastion of conservatism, church building, amidst much mediocrity also generated a number of restorations and new churches which, with great facility, adapted traditional forms to contemporary requirements. Prominent here were H S Goodhart-Rendel and Stephen Dykes Bower, Surveyor to the Fabric at Westminster Abbey from 1951, whose works included the Romanesque St John's, Newbury (1957), and the high altar and baldacchino at St Paul's Cathedral, London (1958). Steeped in the Gothic Revival, Dykes Bower also designed St Vedast's Rectory in the City of London (1959) in a classical style reminiscent of the work of the greatest classicist of the period, Raymond Erith, who was appointed architect for the restoration of 10–12 Downing Street, London, in 1958. The single greatest classical work of the decade was, however, Sir Albert Richardson's Bracken House, Cannon Street, London (1959), built for the *Financial Times* in a style derived from Karl Friedrich Schinkel. Dismissed at the time, it was the first post-war building to be listed. Richardson also played a major role in the controversy over the replanning of the area around St Paul's pressing William Holford, the appointed planner, to adopt a formal setting for the cathedral.

By the late 1950s public concern was mounting at the increasing incidence of tall buildings, both residential and commercial, and the threat posed by uncontrolled speculative development. In housing, in the wake of the abolition of the general needs subsidy in 1956, a new emphasis on slum clearance hastened the trend towards higher blocks to meet density targets in confined inner-city areas. By 1960 proposals for blocks of 19 storeys or more, dwarfing the 16 at Golden Lane, had been approved not just in London but in cities as far apart as Bristol and Glasgow. The stage was set for the 1960s dash for growth through system building which would see the standards attained by many 1950s blocks sacrificed on the altar of quantity. If the building type most characteristic of the decade's early years had been the primary school, that of its closing years was the office building, an increasing number of which were curtain-walled and erected by developers seeking a lucrative return on their investment. These were designed by a relatively small number of architects (including Richard Seifert whose office grew from 12 employees in 1955 to 200 by 1966) who were able to plot a smooth course through the maze of planning regulations which had in any case been relaxed as the decade progressed. The accompanying change in architectural attitude was summed up by Goldfinger: 'The economics of buildings for whomever they are carried out is the ratio of enclosed space to useable [sic] space. This equation means for the developer so much money spent per cubic foot of building, so much money received per square foot of lettable space . . . Somebody should tell the self-styled "socially conscious" architects about the facts of life and jolt them out of their fairyland of make-believe.'[31] With the property boom in full swing, the effectively unchecked activities of speculative developers were thrown into sharp focus by the proposals of one of the most successful, Jack Cotton, to redevelop the Cafe Monico site in Piccadilly Circus. The sheer vulgarity of the designs provoked a public outcry which resulted in a public enquiry and their eventual rejection by the Minister. The Civic Trust, which had been founded in 1957, played a prominent part in opposing the scheme and reflected the growth of an increasingly vociferous and organized conservation lobby horrified by the losses inflicted in the name of comprehensive urban redevelopment. To environmental fears expressed, for example, by Cullen and Nairn's 'Outrage' at spreading 'subtopia'[32] – a no man's land between town and country of visual clutter such as wire fencing, unsightly signage and car parks – could now be added new concerns for the country's specifically architectural heritage evidenced in the Victorian Society's formation in 1958.

As the decade closed, despite John Summerson's advocacy of 'the programme' as Modernism's unifying element,[33] modern architecture remained essentially

Basil Spence. Thorn House, Upper St Martin's Lane, London (1960) Photo: Henk Snoek

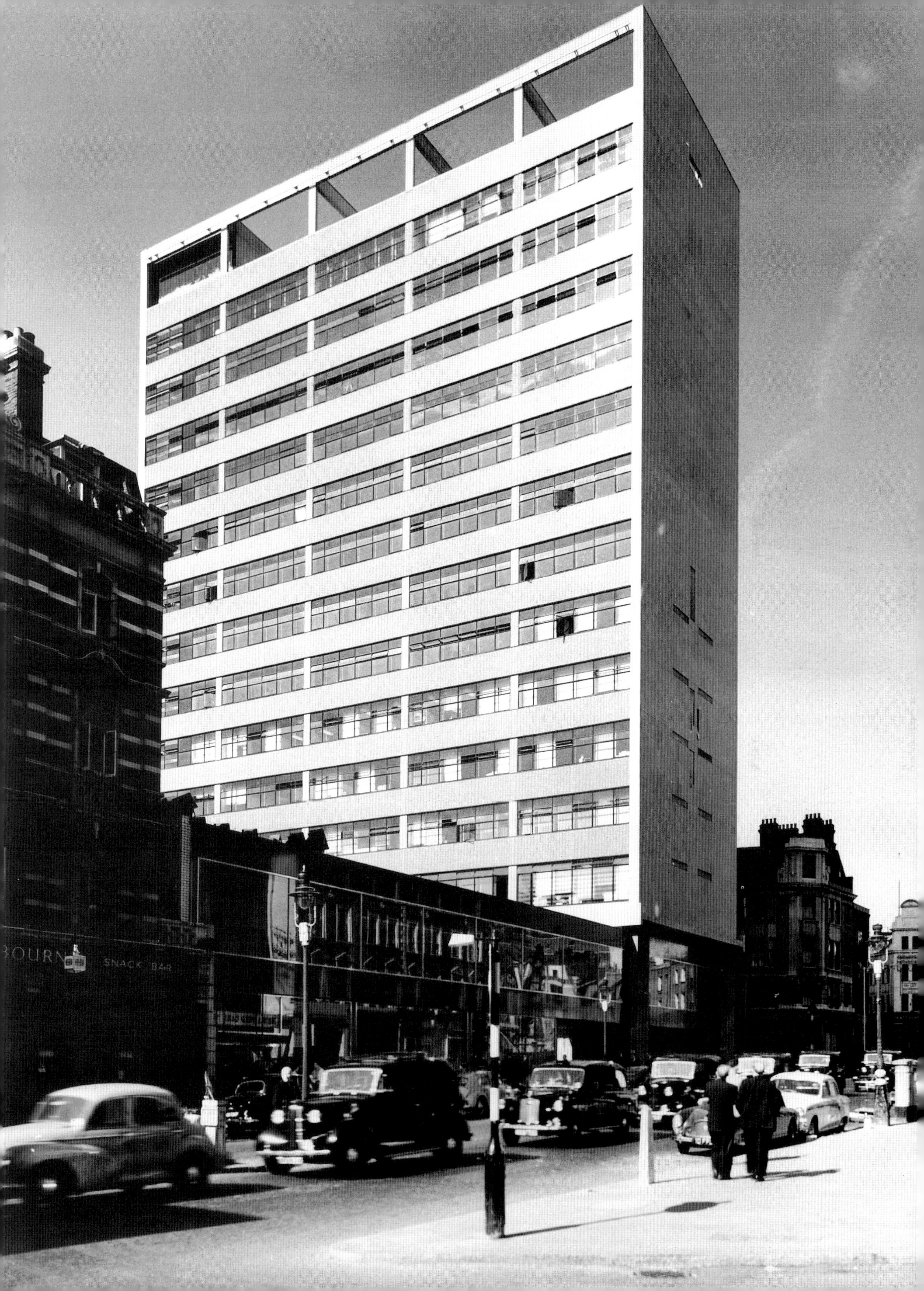
SNACK BAR

disparate in nature. Ranged against those still pursuing a system-built technological nirvana were those architects, dubbed 'The Art Boys' by Leonard Manasseh, for whom the expanded building programmes of the 1960s, especially in university architecture, afforded new opportunities for greater individual expression. In 1966 Pevsner felt impelled to denounce a new cult of personality in architecture[34] – a charge which underlined how far the architectural climate had changed in the decade since the anonymity of public office had been the norm. If technocratically-minded architects such as Donald Gibson epitomized the 1950s, the new era belonged to architectural stars such as Seifert and Stirling. Similarly, if at the beginning of the 1950s the social idealism of Sweden's Welfare State had been a formative influence, by its end American style consumerism was dominant. In 1950 the *Architectural Review* castigated 'Man-made America'; by 1957 it was lauding 'Machine-made America'.[35] Just as in Diana Dors and Tommy Steele Britain had its home-grown versions of Marilyn and Elvis, so in Castrol House and Basil Spence's Thorn House, London, completed in early 1960, it had its echoes of Skidmore Owings & Merrill's Lever Building, New York (1952). These temples of corporate power symbolized the arrival on English shores of what J K Galbraith had termed 'The Affluent Society', the hedonism of which was to make dreams of building a better tomorrow, of constructing a social architecture, seem ever more atavistic.

Notes

1. *Architect & Building News*, vol 197, 6 January 1950, p1.
2. Ascribed to Gerald Barry, Director General of the Festival.
3. Quoted in Mary Banham and Bevis Hillier (eds), *A Tonic to the Nation: the Festival of Britain 1951* (Thames & Hudson: London, 1976), p11.
4. *Architectural Review*, vol 110, August 1951, p80.
5. *Architectural Design*, vol 29, January 1959, p35.
6. See *Architectural Review*, vol 126, July 1959, pp21–35.
7. *Architects' Journal*, vol 117, 8 January 1953, p37.
8. Quoted in Andrew Saint, *Towards a Social Architecture: the Role of School-Building in Post-War England* (Yale University Press: New Haven & London, 1987), p21.
9. *Architects' Journal*, vol 118, 9 July 1953, p39.
10. *Ibid.*, vol 108, 2 December 1948, p505.
11. See *Architectural Review*, vol 101, June 1947, pp199–204 and vol 103, January 1948, pp9–22.
12. *Ibid.*, vol 134, September 1963, pp180–2.
13. Hazel Evans (ed), *New Towns: the British Experience*, (Knight for the Town & Country Planning Association: London, 1972), p96.
14. *Architectural Review*, vol 114, July 1953, pp28–32.
15. *Ibid.*, p33.
16. Talk by Stirrat Johnson-Marshall broadcast by the BBC Third Programme, 11 June 1950, quoted in Andrew Saint, *Towards a Social Architecture*, p251.
17. *Zodiac*, vol 12, 1964, p47.
18. *Architects' Journal*, vol 129, 16 April 1959, p579.
19. Trevor Dannatt, *Modern Architecture in Britain* (Batsford: London, 1959), p27.
20. *Architects' Journal*, vol 124, 19 July 1956, p75.
21. Phrase used by Peter Smithson quoted in David Robbins (ed), *The Independent Group: Postwar Britain and the Aesthetics of Plenty* (MIT Press: Cambridge, Mass. & London, 1990), p242.
22. *Architects' Journal*, vol 126, 12 September 1957, p387.
23. Reyner Banham, *The New Brutalism: Ethic or Aesthetic?* (Architectural Press: London, 1966), p15.
24. *Architects' Journal*, vol 120, 16 September 1954, p335.
25. *Architectural Review*, vol 118, December 1955, p357.
26. *New Statesman*, 19 July 1958.
27. *Architecture & Building*, vol 34, May 1959, p167.
28. *Architectural Review*, vol 121, February 1957, p104.
29. G E Kidder Smith, *The New Architecture of Europe* (Penguin Books: Harmondsworth, 1961), p51.
30. *Twentieth Century*, Winter 1963, p147.
31. *New Statesman*, 10 May 1958.
32. *Architectural Review*, vol 117, June 1955.
33. See John Summerson, 'The Case for a Theory of Modern Architecture', *RIBA Journal*, vol 64, June 1957, pp307–10.
34. Nikolaus Pevsner, *The Anti-Pioneers* radio talks broadcast by the BBC 1956–7.
35. See *Architectural Review*, vol 108, December 1950 and vol 121, May 1957.

The Festival of Britain

The Festival of Britain's ostensible purpose was to celebrate the centenary of the Great Exhibition and to display the British contribution to art, science, technology and industrial design since 1851. Its real aim, like the Philadelphia Centennial of 1876, however, was to boost the morale of a nation wearied by war and the rigours of post-war austerity and to restore faith in the future by providing proof that Britain could indeed 'make it'. Despite shortages of materials, labour and money, and in incredibly quick time, 19 pavilions, 13 cafe-restaurants, a concert hall, cinema and various administrative offices were erected on a small 27 acre site on the South Bank – a tremendous feat of organization and teamwork that owed much to experience gained during the war and the coordinating control of the Design Group and Architectural Council under the chairmanship respectively of Hugh Casson and Howard Lobb. For the first time a large-scale exhibition was planned to tell a sequential story – that of the British Isles and its people – with the individual pavilions being treated as separate chapters in the unfolding narrative. This story-telling approach, which had its origins in the war and the work done by the Ministry of Information, was to dominate British submissions to future international expositions. The design of the individual buildings was entrusted to a new generation of largely untried architects whose average age was under 45 and whose work was characterized by Casson as 'gay, ephemeral, frail and elegant', a suitably 'off-rations' modern antidote to the drabness of post-war existence.

While the extensive use made of glass prefigured the dominance of the glass box type of pavilion at the Brussels Expo in 1958 such as Edward Mills' British Industries Pavilion, no new structural techniques were introduced at the Festival. However, it did afford younger architects, hitherto starved of opportunities, the chance to experiment on a comparatively lavish scale with materials and methods in the main unfamiliar to them. Similarly no new architectural language was born on the South Bank. The influence of the *Exhibition of Modern Industrial and Decorative Arts*, Stockholm (1930), as well as of more recent developments not only in Sweden but also in Italy was clearly discernible, and even Ralph Tubbs, the architect of the Festival's most radical structure, the Dome of Discovery, regarded his work not as something innovative, but as the culmination of what the MARS Group had sought to achieve in the 1930s. If the style itself was not new, however, then the public acceptance it gained as a result of the exhibition certainly was.

Festival of Britain under construction, South Bank, London (1951) *Photo: John Maltby*

As Misha Black, coordinating architect for the upstream section, remarked, 'What had been the private pleasure of a few cognoscenti suddenly virtually overnight achieved enthusiastic public acclaim.'

The true significance of the Festival lay less in its buildings, which a new generation of architects soon dismissed as 'flimsy' and 'effeminate', than in providing the British public with its first experience of an integrated environment created, in the words of the *Architectural Review*, 'wholly in the spirit of modern architecture', and in which as much attention was paid to the space between buildings as to the buildings themselves. The Festival thus offered an alternative to the Beaux-Arts tradition of exhibition planning, the conservatism of which was often at odds with the architecture on show, by adopting a more informal, picturesque approach that emphasized the delights not of the monumental vista but of surprise, contrast and changes in scale and texture. The detailed attention given to all aspects of landscaping, the skilful use of sudden changes in level, the creation in fact of a modern 'townscape' were the triumphs of the exhibition eagerly latched on to by the creators of the New Towns and rebuilders of city centres such as Coventry at home, and the organizers of international exhibitions such as the Montreal Expo 1967 abroad.

▶ The aluminium-plated Skylon, dramatically soaring 250 ft into the air and, as the contemporary joke went, like Britain without visible means of support – in fact it was supported by a complex arrangement of steel cables and splayed pylons – provided the Festival with a highly imaginative and beautiful symbol of the hope that Britain would break free from post-war austerity. Powell & Moya's design, which was chosen from 157 entries in a competition for the Festival's vertical feature, had, as the Archbishop of Canterbury remarked, 'the supreme merit of serving no useful purpose whatsoever' and when the exhibition ended it was dismantled and sold for scrap.

When constructed the Dome of Discovery, 365 ft in diameter and 93 ft high, was the largest dome in the world and appeared to contemporaries as if it had just escaped from a Dan Dare comic strip. Ralph Tubbs later remarked that 'the dome was rather esoteric, using a design based on the poetry of mathematics and requiring a revolutionary structure. It was a triumph of engineering skills [the engineers were Freeman Fox & Partners] which, although suppressed for many years, can now be seen again in the work of high-tech architects'. Like Skylon, the Dome was built of aluminium, a material then in its exploratory stage. The interior, consisting of a series of reinforced concrete galleries, was much less imaginative than the exterior and rather spoilt by the cluttered display.

Powell & Moya. Skylon, Festival of Britain, South Bank, London (1951)
Photo: Colin Westwood

Ralph Tubbs. Dome of Discovery, Festival of Britain, South Bank, London (1951)

THE FESTIVAL OF BRITAIN

Fry Drew & Partners. Thames-side Restaurant, Festival of Britain, South Bank, London (1951)

The Festival saw the introduction of few new structural techniques. One of the more interesting experiments was to be found in the Thames-side Restaurant, designed by Maxwell Fry and Jane Drew, the roof of which comprised a double skin of aluminium with a cork sandwich which could be speedily assembled on site by using methods customarily employed in riveting aircraft. The idea for this had suggested itself to the architects when cooperating with several aircraft factories on the manufacture of prefabricated kitchens. The jaunty, nautical style of the restaurant, particularly evident in its railings, boardwalk and striped awning, exuded an appropriately festive air.

The Lion & Unicorn Pavilion was a rare instance at the Festival of both structure and display within being designed by the same team. R D Russell and R Y Goodden had been involved in the *Britain Can Make It* exhibition in 1946 and their pavilion, which resembled a Dutch barn, was the one building besides the Dome of Discovery to be frankly expressed as an envelope for exhibits. The chief features of its well-proportioned exterior were the arched lamella oak roof (wood while indispensable for display was otherwise little used in the buildings on the South Bank as it was in such short supply) and the distinctive series of eye-shaped windows. The pavilion's display on the British character was described by Misha Black as 'a delicious romp'.

R D Russell & R Y Goodden. Lion & Unicorn Pavilion, Festival of Britain, South Bank, London (1951)
Photos: Colin Westwood

Each of the exhibition's coordinating architects awarded himself one building to design. Misha Black chose the Regatta Restaurant and the decoration of the Bailey Bridge over the Thames, executed in conjunction with Alexander Gibson, one of Black's associates in the Design Research Unit. The restaurant epitomized the Festival's attempts, not entirely successful, to unify architecture and art, Black writing, 'I set out to show how a building could be a neutral *ambience* for the work of artists'. These included Victor Pasmore, John Tunnard and Laurence Scarfe while the garden boasted *Cypress*, a sculpture by Lynn Chadwick. The restaurant also exemplified many townscape features including changes in level to provide differing views and an informal arrangement of sculpture, planting and water to give textural variety and counterbalance the strict geometry of the architecture.

As the *Architectural Review* remarked, the Festival details – lettering, signage, furniture, wallscape, planting, etc – were of a remarkably high standard providing 'an object lesson to town-planners, borough engineers and others responsible for the design of roads and their furniture, public spaces and their layout, and of all the other incidentals that occupy the foreground of the urban landscape'. Of particular note were Ernest Race's Antelope chairs and Maria Shepherd's plant pots which quickly became ubiquitous symbols of the 'Contemporary' style.

Misha Black and Alexander Gibson. Regatta Restaurant, Festival of Britain, South Bank, London (1951) *Photo: Colin Westwood*

Festival of Britain, South Bank, London (1951) *Photo: John Maltby*

THE FESTIVAL OF BRITAIN

Education

During the 1950s educational building was concentrated largely on primary and secondary provision with the explosion in tertiary education occurring in the 1960s. In the wake of the 1944 Education Act which, by raising the school leaving age to 15, introduced secondary education for all, local authorities were charged with providing schools for a greatly increased number of children – a number which was to be swollen still further by the post-war baby boom. In order to meet this urgent need many authorities were forced to erect huts under the prosaically named Hutting Operation for Raising the School Leaving Age (HORSA). The problem was especially acute in the small Conservative-controlled county of Hertfordshire as it contained within its boundaries four designated New Towns and several London overspill estates. In 1946 it was calculated that it would need to build 175 schools in 15 years. While it had little option but to adopt HORSA for many of its secondary schools, under the enlightened supervision of its chief education officer, John Newsom, and newly appointed county architect, C H Aslin, Hertfordshire developed a programme for its primary schools which was radical both in conception and implementation and which resulted in schools which Walter Gropius acclaimed in 1952 as the most advanced in the world. This programme, underpinned by an unwavering concern for social justice allied to a strong commitment to the new ideas of child-centred learning, was largely devised by Aslin's deputy, Stirrat Johnson-Marshall, and the eager young team he assembled which included among its leading lights, David Medd and his wife-to-be, Mary Crowley.

From the outset it was obvious that prefabrication would be necessary to build the requisite number of schools. However, for the usual prefabrication of whole buildings or large units the Hertfordshire team innovatively substituted the prefabrication of components thereby building up a stock of standard, interchangeable parts which could be assembled according to differing requirements. In this way it was not only hoped to avoid the monotony usually associated with prefabrication but, more importantly, to devise a new vocabulary of school building from which all could benefit. The Hertfordshire strategy which conceived of school building in terms of a developing programme rather than a series of unrelated one-offs enabled the team to establish close links with sympathetic manufacturers who in turn were assured of a sufficient

**London County Council Architects Department.
Primary school, Dulwich, London (1953)**
Photo: John Pantlin

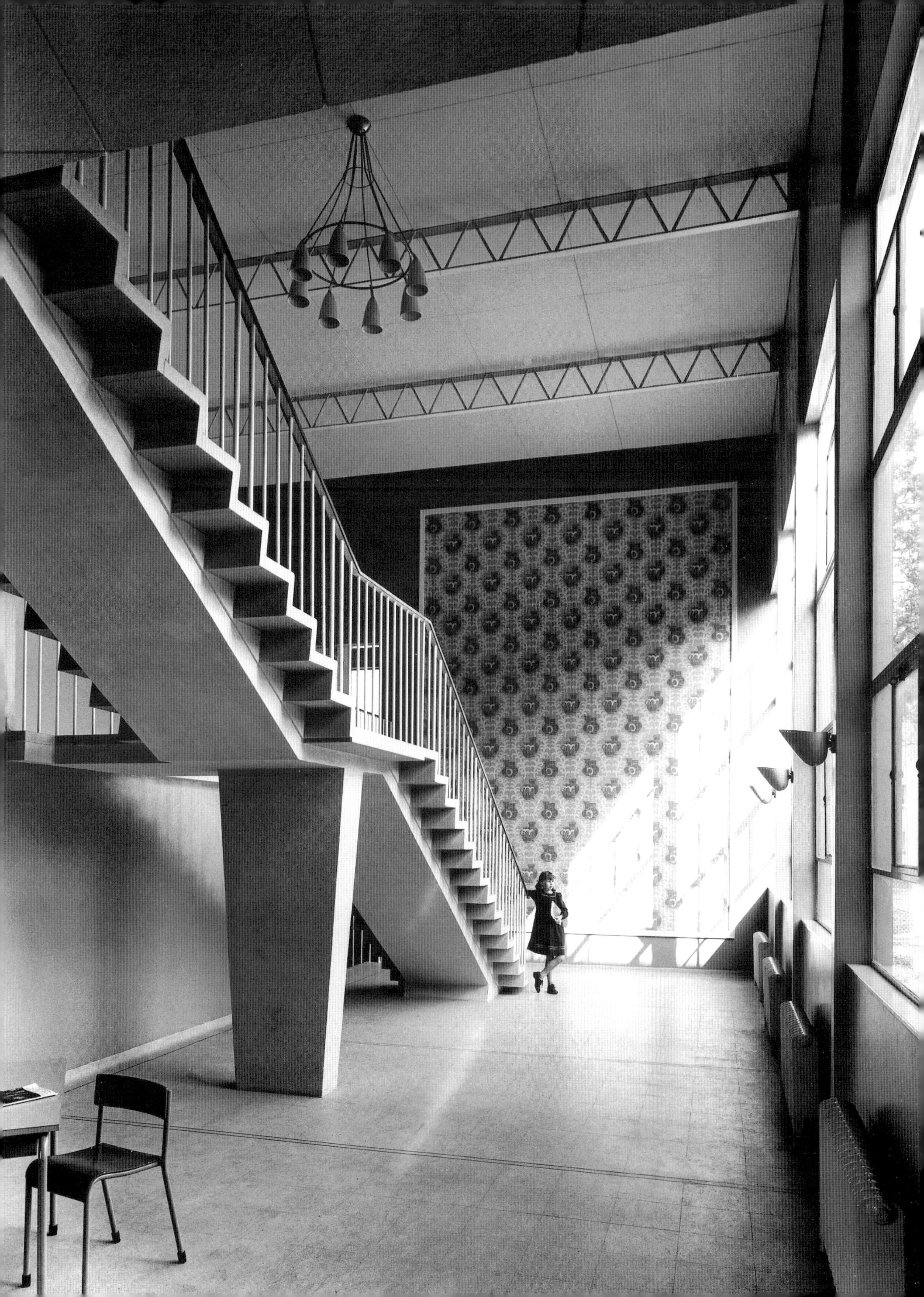

volume of ongoing work to guarantee their continued commitment to the programme. Also of vital importance was the close liaison with educationalists who contributed to the detailed research and analysis undertaken before design and then provided feedback on particular schools once built which could be used to improve later ones. Most important of all was the emphasis on group working and the use of collaborative skills honed during wartime which were necessary to meet the programme's tight deadlines. While individually most of these working methods were not new, the Hertfordshire approach was novel in its combination and thoroughgoing application of them to a single end.

Wishing to transfer his ideas to the national scene, Johnson-Marshall left Hertfordshire in 1948 to become chief architect to the Ministry of Education where he was subsequently joined by former Hertfordshire colleagues such as the Medds. The methodology introduced at Hertfordshire, however, proved sufficiently sound for the authority to continue to produce good schools even after the completion in 1949–50 of the schools Johnson-Marshall had initiated. With Hertfordshire focusing on primary school provision, the Ministry tackled the thornier issue of secondary schools, for which, apart from the grammar school, no adequate models existed. It built five prototypes, the most influential of which was Wokingham. The Ministry's other main contributions were the issuing of its practically informative *Building Bulletins* and the development of rigorous methods of cost analysis and planning.

The collaborative and developmental nature of school building pioneered at Hertfordshire reached its apogee in the formal establishment of the Consortium of Local Authorities Special Programme (CLASP) in 1957 which had originated two years earlier in attempts by Nottinghamshire to devise a system capable of withstanding the effects of subsidence caused by mining. As Nottinghamshire lacked by itself a sufficiently large school programme to justify production costs, the result was CLASP – the first cooperative venture between local authorities, all with subsidence problems, to build schools using the methods conceived in Nottinghamshire and thereby achieve significant economies of scale. The success of the system was such that it later spread to other building types and its full-scale school erected at the Milan Triennale in 1960 was awarded a Special Grand Prize – a fitting tribute not just to CLASP but to the excellence of British post-war school building generally.

As the Hertfordshire architects had insufficient time to develop a prototype school of their own they adopted a ready-made solution in the light steel (or 'Meccano' as David Medd dubbed it) system devised in line with government recommendations by Hills & Company of West Bromwich. The first schools to use the system were the concrete-clad Burleigh School, Cheshunt, and Essendon, both with Scandinavian overtones but with the latter a much tighter composition. Henry Swain, then a student but later to join Hertfordshire, recalled to the historian Andrew Saint, 'I can't impress on you too much how different these buildings looked. Seen in the context of the Modern Movement, everything monstrous and big and reinforced, here was something light and delicate and hammered out of the process of studying the problem.'

The Hills system was thoroughly revised by Medd in 1947 and thereafter on an annual basis as were the schools' individual structural components and pieces of equipment. Particularly important was the adoption of the more flexible 'grid' rather than 'bay' arrangement of prefabrication which allowed greater variations in scale and internal planning. As the programme evolved, the primitivism of Burleigh and Essendon was replaced by an increasing sophistication and, following the introduction of cost limits in 1950, by more compact planning which saw classroom sizes actually increased by ingeniously grouping them in pairs, eliminating corridors and reducing circulation space to a minimum.

Hertfordshire County Architects Department. Burleigh School, Cheshunt (1948)
Photo: Colin Westwood

Hertfordshire County Architects Department. Construction of primary school, Leavesden (1949) Photo: John Maltby

EDUCATION 33

Hertfordshire County Architects Department. Primary school, Essendon (1948) *Photo: John Maltby*

▶ The Hertfordshire schools were also distinguished by their seeming informality of plan and detailing; by their lighting, especially daylighting made possible by generous window provision; by the use of strong primary colours in conscious reaction to the drab wartime camouflage hues of khaki and bottle green; and by their incorporation of enlivening works of art, especially murals. Although the 8 ft 3 in module was adopted by authorities such as the LCC for its primary schools and the use of some individual components developed at Hertfordshire such as Adamsez basins and Percon light fittings did become widespread, Hertfordshire's ultimate aspiration to create a universally applicable architectural language based on standardized, interchangeable components went unrealized. The module itself proved more inflexible than first thought, the structural components were specific to the Hertfordshire system, and in practice there turned out to be many individual variations from school to school which demanded on-site solutions. The Spartan elevations, derived in part from the aesthetic limitations of the system and in part from the decision, when funds were limited, to give priority to the provision of amenities, make it hard for us today to appreciate what a great step forward these airy, light schools represented over their usually intimidating and Stygian forbears and how revolutionary they were, not least in unequivocally demonstrating that Modernism, scientifically and sensitively applied, was capable of creating a humane environment responsive to children's needs.

Hertfordshire County Architects Department. Classroom, Burleigh School, Cheshunt (1948)

34 BUILDING A BETTER TOMORROW

Ministry of Education Architects' and Building Branch. St Crispin's Secondary Modern School, Wokingham (1953) Photo: John Maltby

▶ The five articles allotted to it by the *Architects' Journal* and the fact that it was one of the few schools to have a Ministry of Education *Building Bulletin* devoted to it attest to the importance of Wokingham School, the first built by the Development Group of the Ministry's Architects' and Building Branch. Designed by David and Mary Medd and Michael Ventris in close collaboration with educationalists, it drew on the Medds' Hertfordshire experience to explore whether the solutions adopted there for single-storey primary schools could be developed and applied to the more vexed problem of multi-storey secondary school provision. In particular it aimed 'to develop a means whereby, especially in areas where site labour is scarce, secondary schools can be built to the standards required in the Building Regulations, at a greater speed than is at present normal, and within the current limits of nett cost'. The school was built to a 3 ft 4 in horizontal and 2 ft vertical module using a hot-rolled steel prefabricated system devised by Hills & Company. This was never developed commercially and, despite some technical innovations such as the introduction of studded rubber flooring, Wokingham was more important educationally than architecturally – a point underlined by its informal plan which was allowed to grow out of 'the educational needs and activities of each of its parts'. As such it was a much studied model of the possible form a distinctive secondary school might take.

Slater Uren & Pike. Kidbrooke Comprehensive School, Corelli Road, Eltham, London (1954)
Photo: John Maltby

▶ The unremitting pace of school building was such that many hard-pressed local authorities farmed out part of their programmes to private architects. Noteworthy examples of schools conceived in this fashion included Ernö Goldfinger's Brandlehow Road Primary School, Wandsworth (1951), and Westville Road Primary School, Hammersmith (1951), for which he designed his own prefabricated concrete construction system. Like these, Kidbrooke formed part of the LCC's programme being not only its first comprehensive school to open but also one of the best, successfully resolving the most difficult problem facing the comprehensive school architect – how to plan a large school yet still retain a sense of humanity and intimacy. Thus despite having to accommodate 2,000 pupils, Kidbrooke was meticulously scaled to children's requirements with finishes of a high standard for 1954 reflecting the fact that planning had begun several years earlier when cost limits were higher. Of most structural interest was the vast, domed assembly hall, the boundary walls of which were post-tensioned using the Freyssinet system. The achievement of Kidbrooke is all the more remarkable when compared to some of the LCC's own comprehensives such as Strand Comprehensive (1956), now Tulse Hill. Here classrooms were packed into a crushingly intimidating nine-storey slab block in what seemed a deliberately provocative rejection of the values espoused by Hertfordshire and the Ministry of Education which the council felt had limited application in the inner city.

Hunstanton School, for which the Smithsons won the commission in 1950 in an open competition assessed by the school architect, Denis Clarke Hall, represents in many respects the antithesis of the Hertfordshire school building programme. Its compact, symmetrical plan, centred on a double-height hall bordered by a pair of inner courts, with classrooms concentrated on the upper floor and circulation and services below, rejected the typical low-spread Hertfordshire approach. The school was designed not as a prototype but as a one-off which, particularly through its brick-infilling, sought to impart an air of permanence the Smithsons felt most prefabricated schools lacked. It also abjured modular construction in favour of an assemblage of off-the-peg components including the Braithwate water tower which came to symbolize the school and presaged High-Tech architecture. The Smithsons' insistence on purity of design resulted in the omission of elements deemed unnecessary, such as glazing sub-frames, so the structure itself became both architecture and ornament. Above all, repudiating the anonymous teamwork which characterized the Hertfordshire programme, Hunstanton represented a reassertion of personal design sensibility expressed in a ruthlessly powerful architectural statement which still awes today. Its structure of welded steel H-frames, designed according to Plastic Theory and chosen to permit the maximum amount of glazing and thus light, was greatly influenced by Mies van der Rohe's Minerals and Metals Research Building, Illinois Institute of Technology, Chicago (1943), while the classical formality of its plan was 'Palladian via Wittkower'.

**Alison & Peter Smithson.
Secondary school under construction, King's Lynn Road, Hunstanton (1954)**
Photos: E E Swain

▶ Peter Smithson recalled, 'I think we saw the building as having two lives, the life of everyday – chalk, dust and kids shouting – and another life when the building is empty, a life of pure space'. It could be argued that while it succeeded in the latter, it failed in the more important former. The structural faults of the school have been well documented – its glazing failures; its steel corroded by salt sea winds; its uncomfortable thermal extremes; its high noise level exacerbated by exposed materials and a plan which obliged children changing classes to go up and down the ten internal staircases. In addition, the architects were unfamiliar with the site and rarely met their client – a factor which enabled the design to survive intact. Despite all this, Hunstanton's status as a building of international import remains undiminished. Fêted on completion by American architect Philip Johnson and swiftly adopted by Banham as the flagship of the crystallizing New Brutalism, Hunstanton strikingly underlines the potency of visual imagery in architecture. While in photographs of Hertfordshire schools the pupils are often included, at Hunstanton the Smithsons even ordered the removal of all furniture to ensure Maltby's compelling images depicted the logical purity of their design. It is images like these which have helped ensure Hunstanton remains *de rigeur* for inclusion in architectural textbooks in a way the more successfully planned but often visually impoverished Hertfordshire schools have not.

Alison & Peter Smithson. Secondary school, King's Lynn Road, Hunstanton (1954) *Photos: John Maltby*

Nottinghamshire County Architects Department. Barnby Road County Infants School, Newark (1958)
Photo: W E Middleton & Son Ltd

On his appointment as Nottinghamshire's county architect in 1955 Donald Gibson set up a development group very much in the image of Hertfordshire, including as it did some of its former key personnel such as Dan Lacey and Henry Swain, to formulate a school building system which would enable the county to improve a poor record made worse by skilled labour shortages and mining subsidence. With concrete construction rejected as too rigid for subsidence sites, the system developed drew on the type of cold rolled steel frame construction then being used by the Ministry for its school at Belper. This was manufactured by John Brockhouse & Company whom Gibson knew from his time as Coventry's chief architect. The main features of the 3 ft 4 in modular system, which was stabilized by spring-loaded diagonal wind braces, were its pin-jointed frame and vibrating roller base earning it the nickname of the 'rock and roll' system. The formation of CLASP and the system's widespread application beyond subsidence sites resulted in cost reductions achieved by standardization of components across participating authorities and by serial contracting which encouraged contractors to submit more competitive tenders. Barnby Road is a typical early CLASP school illustrating the system's use of a wider range of external materials than the concrete cladding and glass infill panels customary at Hertfordshire. Here, as there was little prospect of vandalism in an infants' school, tiled cladding was used throughout.

**Gollins Melvin Ward & Partners.
Library, Sheffield University,
Sheffield (1959)**
Photo: Henk Snoek

Success in the open competition to design the central areas of an expanding Sheffield University in 1953 brought Gollins Melvin Ward & Partners to architectural prominence and began a long association with the university. The library, designed to house a million books and therefore one of the largest in Britain, was the first part of the central complex to be built, being opened by T S Eliot in 1959. It took the form of a low square to contrast with the 17-storey arts block completed by the same architects in 1965. The geometric precision of its exterior was echoed inside by the crisp detailing and clear circulation pattern. Lavish materials like marble were used in the public areas and it was the country's first large library to be designed with air filtration and temperature and humidity controls. However, it was soon apparent that the brief to which the architects had strictly adhered had become outdated. The explosion in student numbers more than doubled the required reader spaces while the proportion of open to closed access stacks proved too low and the intake of volumes far greater than anticipated. The problem was compounded by the library's inherent rigidity which made conversion difficult – a point noted by library architects during the great university expansion of the 1960s where the emphasis was on flexibility. Even so the library's qualities were such that Pevsner hailed it 'the best individual twentieth-century building of Sheffield'.

Housing

In 1945 it was estimated that 475,000 houses had either been destroyed or rendered uninhabitable by enemy action. The scale and urgency of the housing problem, exacerbated by a rising population and the existence of many substandard dwellings, demanded greater governmental involvement in this field than ever before and the new Labour government was in any case ideologically committed to state provision of decent housing as one of the key elements of its Welfare State programme. The Conservatives followed this lead with Minister of Housing and Local Government Harold Macmillan's generous subsidies enabling home building to peak in 1954. Of the impressive number of 2.5 million dwellings built between 1945 and 1957, therefore, three-quarters was public housing provided either directly by local authorities with, from 1950, the LCC in the van, or by private architects commissioned by them.

What is immediately striking about this period of domestic architecture is the diversity of housing types. Not only did new forms appear, such as the maisonette block introduced by Powell & Moya at Pimlico, but there was also a serious attempt to re-invigorate urban dwelling as a coherently planned and compact antidote to the dreaded ribbon development and unfettered sprawl of the semi during the inter-war years. This meant a significant increase in flat building to achieve higher densities and free up surrounding land for productive or leisure use. The form and disposition of these flats was intensely debated especially once the country's first point block had been built by Gibberd at Harlow in 1951 which constituted a challenge to the *Zeilenbau* or row layout seen, for example, at Tecton's Spa Green Estate. The ensuing point versus slab block argument was eventually resolved by the use of the former for small dwellings and the latter for those of medium size.

While the majority of flats were in blocks of three to four storeys, it was the increasingly tall blocks, such as that at Golden Lane, built with the intention of catering for the growing number of one or two person households, which, though small in number, attracted most attention. Such blocks usually formed part of mixed development schemes, a new concept espoused during the period which rested on the belief that by mixing dwelling types – house, flats and maisonettes – on the same estate, greater visual interest and, more importantly, a balanced development with a cross-section of all classes could be achieved. Mixed development, first systematically implemented by Gibberd at Shacklewell Road and Somerford Grove, Hackney (1947), and most eloquently championed at Alton East, was therefore a form of social engineering as

John Bickerdike. 8 Ashley Close, Welwyn Garden City (1953) *Photo: John Pantlin*

well as an attempt to match dwelling size to type of household. Despite continued resistance to flat living and some financially driven reductions in space standards, these flats, which were for the most part thoughtfully planned and well-equipped with modern amenities, proved generally popular with tenants representing as they did, especially in the design of their kitchens and bathrooms, a significant improvement on pre-war standards.

The achievement of British public housing during the decade was such for it justly to be considered among the finest anywhere. However, the abolition of the subsidy for dwellings for general needs in 1956 and reliance on the private sector to fill the void, combined with a poor record of slum clearance, saw the decade end with the onset of a new housing crisis. This was to be tackled in the 1960s by an increased emphasis on quantity at the expense of quality seen through the extensive adoption of system-built tower blocks and the growing tendency to house families in such blocks.

This resulted in worsening social problems and widespread disenchantment with the supposed benefits of the vertical garden city.

With the exception of Span and individual developments such as Stirling & Gowan's flats at Ham Common, speculative housing of the period generally continued to be of a low standard. Of more interest architecturally was the revival, after the abolition of licences, in the building of one-off houses. Common features of the most innovative examples of these included the prevalence of open-planning reflecting a new domestic informality; heightened interplay between interior and exterior made possible by the growing use of the picture window; employment of a much wider range of materials both externally and internally resulting in much richer effects than had been common in modernist houses of the 1930s; and an increased awareness of the importance of colour, texture and planting in creating a homely environment.

▶ After brief flirtations with the point block such as the nine-storey The Lawn, and the slab block seen in Yorke Rosenberg & Mardall's Sish Lane, Stevenage (1952), most New Town housing took the form of brick terraces with low pitched roofs. Reflecting inhabitants' expressed desires for houses with gardens, flats were rare – comprising 10 to 20 per cent of housing in areas of Harlow and only 5 per cent at Crawley – and the densities achieved low, fuelling criticism that these were suburbs disguised as towns. At Harlow the housing was executed by Gibberd, by private firms such as Powell & Moya and H T Cadbury-Brown, and by some use, at Ministry insistence, of system building such as Wimpey's 'no fines' concrete house. Characteristic of its housing was the open front in preference to the enclosed private garden which was instead sited at the rear, screened from view. Where two terraces met at right angles the rear gardens were hidden by small corner flat blocks designed to harmonize with the adjacent terraces. Faced with the housing shortage, the government's tendency was to put an exaggerated emphasis on house building in the New Towns at the expense of the social and work facilities required to make them the wholly self-contained entities they were planned to be. This led to criticism that they were themselves becoming the very dormitory suburbs they had been designed to prevent.

Frederick Gibberd. The Lawn, Harlow (1951)

Mark Hall North, Harlow (1959)
Photos: John McCann

HOUSING 43

Tecton; executive architects Skinner & Lubetkin. Spa Green Estate, Rosebery Avenue, London (1950)
Photo: John Maltby

▶ Planned before the war, Spa Green was fundamentally redesigned to take account of the enlargement of the site by bombing, the stipulations of the *County of London Plan*, and post-war stringencies. The design that emerged, and which was completed after Tecton's dissolution in 1948, was a significant improvement not least because in the interim Arup had designed a revolutionary system of box-frame concrete construction which Lubetkin adopted. Using a Danish shuttering method, not only did this result in considerable economies but also, by freeing the elevations of structural constraints, it allowed Lubetkin to explore elevational treatments which he hoped would restore the facade's emotional and visual impact. He felt such impact had been ignored by many modernist architects whose fetishistic insistence that form inexorably followed function had resulted in exteriors of monotonous anonymity. Lubetkin found his solution in the chequerboard motif, here expressed in a rhythmic refrain of contrasting colours, balconies and brickwork, and explored further in later schemes. Critics, such as Julius Posener in a 1951 article in *Architectural Design* entitled 'Knots in the Master's Carpet', accused Lubetkin of formalism and an obsession with pattern-making which seemed to confirm his increasing estrangement from the architectural mainstream. The flats, however, which escaped the harsher rigours imposed on later estates such as Priory Green (1952), were spacious and well equipped, especially the kitchens which incorporated the first use in London of the Garchey waste disposal system.

Holford Square was part of the major revival of Finsbury's housing stock carried out by Lubetkin and Tecton for its progressive Metropolitan Borough Council. However, unlike its predecessors, the Spa Green and Priory Green estates, both planned before the war as part of a major slum clearance programme, the redevelopment of Holford Square was made necessary by the destruction of many of its late-Regency buildings by bombing. Lubetkin greatly admired the square and its neighbourhood and his original intention therefore was to preserve its form. This scheme, however, was rejected on cost grounds and the estate as built filled the square rather than embraced it. Lubetkin provided 130 dwellings in two blocks: 12 in the smaller Holford House and 118 in the main block, Bevin Court, the Y-shape of which was Lubetkin's first built example of a form which had fascinated him since his earliest student days. With balconies ruled out as too expensive, Bevin Court relied, not altogether successfully, on surface patterning to enliven its facade. Inside, however, the story was very different with a mural by Peter Yates providing the appetizer for one of Lubetkin's most extraordinarily dramatic spatial and sculptural creations – the main staircase. Here was the realization of a Piranesian fantasy, a homage to the *Carceri*, at once thrilling and foreboding.

Tecton, developed and executed by Skinner Bailey & Lubetkin with A Green. Housing, Holford Square, London (1954) *Photo: John Maltby*

Powell & Moya, then 25 and 26 respectively, won the competition for Churchill Gardens in 1946. As the client, Westminster City Council, decided to concentrate the bulk of its housing programme in one area, the estate was on a massive scale and presented a daunting task to two such young architects. Built in four sections between 1948 and 1962, it comprised staggered, tall slab blocks of flats set largely at right angles to the Thames, interspersed with lower blocks of maisonettes and three-storey houses disposed parallel to the river. The design of the individual blocks was modified as building progressed. Whereas, for example, the blocks in Section 1 had lift and staircase access, Westminster's requirement for a larger number of smaller flats in Section 2 dictated balcony access. Criticized for its bleakness and cramped feel resulting from the blocks being sited too closely together, the estate was nevertheless pioneering in many respects, not least in its provision of district heating fuelled by refuse from Battersea Power Station across the river. It also set an extremely influential precedent for the spate of high-density housing schemes which followed. It is all the more ironic, therefore, that as the estate was nearing completion, construction of Darbourne & Darke's nearby Lillington Gardens Estate, which demonstrated that comparable densities could be achieved by more acceptable low-rise schemes, was just getting under way.

Powell & Moya. Churchill Gardens, Pimlico, London
Photo (ext, 1954): John Pantlin
Photo (children's playground, 1956): John Maltby

BUILDING A BETTER TOMORROW

In the tranquil surroundings of south Norfolk Tayler & Green produced some of the best post-war housing, distinguished by its responsiveness to locale and landscape and by a commonsense but imaginative use of traditional materials, which avoided sham folksiness on the one hand and the temptation to make an architectural statement *à la* Hunstanton School nearby on the other. Their achievement must be set in the context of English rural housing, much of which was appallingly substandard, and efforts to ameliorate it, which were generally denounced by critics like Nairn and Cullen dismayed by spreading 'subtopia'. After their appointment as its architects in 1944, Tayler & Green formulated a large number of standard housing types and details for their enlightened patrons, Loddon Rural District Council. These revealed a preference for terraced housing rather than the ubiquitous semi, Tayler writing, 'the simple long line of a terrace looks somehow less impertinent in the landscape than a row of pointed teeth with alternate teeth extracted'. Reduced ceiling heights, shallow pitched roofs and pantiles emphasized the horizontality of these terraces allowing them to meld into the landscape's natural contours. The provision of wide frontages and through access from front to back gardens together with the creative use of colour and decorative brick patterning helped overcome resistance to terraced housing and give, in Sherban Cantacuzino's words, 'a quality which in council housing is unique in England, the fine quality of pictorial composition'.

Tayler & Green. Housing, Loddon, Norfolk (1955)

Tayler & Green. 1–16 The Boltons, Hales, Norfolk (1955)
Photos: John McCann

HOUSING 47

London County Council Architects Department. Alton East Estate, Roehampton, London (1955)

▶ The two adjacent estates of Alton East and Alton West, which together formed one of the largest and most important housing developments in Europe, are striking testaments to the idealism and social commitment of members of the London County Council Architects Department. At the same time in their radically different approaches they encapsulate not only the fevered, ideologically disputatious atmosphere within the LCC in those heady years but also wider debates about housing form and the very nature of English Modernism. When control of London's housing programme was finally wrested from the LCC's valuer in 1950, the newly formed LCC Housing Division was determined to break away from the walk-up tenement which had characterized London housing in the immediate post-war period. The solution now, as recommended by Abercrombie and Forshaw in *The County of London Plan* (1943) was to be mixed development, first tried out on the Ackroyden Estate (1952) but given mature expression at Alton East by a group of architects headed by Rosemary Stjernstedt and including Oliver Cox and Cleeve Barr. Their design, with its emphasis on informal layout, varied forms and picturesque landscaping, was heavily influenced by Swedish models such as Vällingby then being developed by Sven Markelius. For this reason, these adherents of the 'New Empiricism' were dubbed by their opponents 'the Swedes' or 'the Softs'.

**London County Council
Architects Department.
Alton East Estate, Roehampton,
London (1955)**
*Photo: London County Council Architects
Department. Photographic Unit*

Built between 1952 and 1955, Alton East consisted of a mixture of flats, maisonettes and houses laid out to take full advantage of the picturesque heavily wooded site. The flats, which accounted for 58 per cent of the total number of dwellings, were arranged in ten 11-storey point blocks, a form of high-rise already introduced into similarly sylvan, and therefore 'sensitive', surroundings by Gibberd at The Lawn, Harlow, and used previously by the LCC at Ackroyden. Here the choice of the point block was determined by the desire to preserve as many trees as possible and by the sloping nature of the site. In contrast to Ackroyden, where the complicated T-shaped plan of the blocks only allowed three flats to a floor, at Alton East the more economical square-shape permitted four. The point block remained a favourite element in the LCC's later housing developments as did the four-storey maisonette block also used here after its successful introduction by Powell & Moya at Churchill Gardens. The maisonettes and terraced houses each had a private garden and gently pitched roofs – a feature which together with the use of brick facing and differing bright colours as visual accents was caustically styled 'People's detailing' in an arcane reference to some of the design team's Communist leanings.

HOUSING   49

London County Council Architects Department. Alton West Estate, Roehampton, London (1959)
Photo: Hugh de Burgh Galwey

▶ Alton West, although sharing a number of characteristics with its companion such as mixed development, use of point blocks and achievement of a similar density, marked a deliberate repudiation of the philosophy underlying Alton East. The 'Hards', among them Colin Lucas, John Partridge and Bill Howell, were, by the time building began in 1954, in the ascendancy. The picturesque sentimentality of Alton East was to be replaced by a more rigorous formalism which looked for its inspiration not to Sweden but to Le Corbusier. This new approach can be seen in the treatment of the point blocks which, in contrast to those at Alton East, had no projections or recessions but were completely flat, while the four-storey maisonette blocks and single-storey old people's houses both had flat rather than pitched roofs. The entirely new feature, however, was the five 11-storey slab blocks of narrow-fronted maisonettes on pilotis, their rough concrete finish and cellular structure derived from Le Corbusier's Unité d'Habitation, Marseilles; their staggered arrangement perhaps from Gropius and Fry's proposal for an Isokon estate at St Leonard's Hill, Windsor (1935). Le Corbusier's influence also extended to the system of dimensional coordination – a variant of *Le Modulor* codenamed 'Charley' to conceal its use from prying 'Softs' – used to try to ensure the high and low blocks related in scale to one another.

Acclaimed by the critic George Kidder Smith as 'probably the finest low cost housing development in the world', the Alton Estate, like the Hertfordshire schools before it, quickly became a hallowed place of architectural pilgrimage. Visitors were rightly impressed by the estate's visual variety and the way its buildings were sensitively related to the attractive landscape. Nor could any doubt its architects' unwavering commitment to provide decent affordable housing for all – a point endorsed by the estate's initial popularity with its 9,500 residents. However, even as the estate was being completed, Park Hill, rising in Sheffield to the designs of J L Womersley, Jack Lynn and Ivor Smith, presented a new housing paradigm which rejected mixed development. Similarly *Architectural Design*, among others, questioned the very notion of mixed development as the supposed correspondence between family type and dwelling size broke down in the face of tenants' actual living patterns. The estate's faults, which are easy to criticize with hindsight, are those with which we have now become all too depressingly familiar on estates up and down the country – isolation from amenities and work opportunities; alienating communal areas; poor maintenance; vandalism. The architects' dream of a new social order created on the drawing board foundered on the hard rock of reality.

London County Council Architects Department. Alton West Estate, Roehampton, London (1959)
Photo: London County Council Architects Department. Photographic Unit

The 1951 competition for the Golden Lane Estate, intended to rehouse City dwellers made homeless by bombing, attracted 178 entries and its assessor, the traditionalist Donald McMorran, chose Geoffrey Powell as the winner. Fulfilling the terms of a pre-competition pact, Powell took into partnership two of his fellow lecturers at the Kingston School of Art, Peter Chamberlin and Christoph Bon, thereby creating what was to become one of Britain's most successful post-war practices. As Powell himself explained when the estate, though unfinished, was formally opened in 1957, it 'aimed at being urban and does not pretend that it is out in the country' and was 'inward looking', deliberately shunning its unattractive surroundings. Golden Lane was thus an urban village, a hard landscaped pedestrian precinct which the *Architectural Review* considered a 'first-rate illustration of the fact that architecture is concerned just as much with space around buildings as with the buildings themselves'. The concentration of 120 flats in the main 16-storey block of Great Arthur House freed up land to be cleverly exploited in a series of changing levels and surprise vistas which effectively demonstrated the estate's townscape qualities. Golden Lane also helped to make fashionable the maisonette, one of the most noteworthy aspects of its internal planning being the way in which additional space was gained in the living rooms of the three-room maisonettes by inclusion within them of the stairwells.

**Chamberlin Powell & Bon.
Golden Lane Estate, City of London, London (1957)**
Photos: John Maltby

BUILDING A BETTER TOMORROW

In his low-cost Bethnal Green housing schemes at Usk Street (1955) and Claredale Street Lasdun developed his 'cluster' alternative to the slab and point block, which he considered too anonymous, overly diagrammatic and, in seeking to apply general solutions to particular problems, unrelated to their specific urban context. In this approach he received theoretical support from the American urban planner Kevin Lynch, who spoke of the city's 'grain' or structure and 'cluster' defined as 'the expression of a unit of natural aggregation' which could be realized in built form by the creation of 'an image of an integrated community'. This was Lasdun's aim in his 14-storey Claredale Street block which was organized on a split-butterfly plan and consisted mostly of stacked maisonettes arranged in four angled wings which were connected by bridges to a free-standing central core containing services and communal amenities. Repudiating the street-deck typology of the Unité, the block was conceived as a vertical street visually reflecting the existing urban grain and recreating the social cohesion of the surrounding neighbourhood. The dwellings were also arranged in small groups so tenants could identify their own particular homes. However, Lasdun's claim that the block thus encouraged community living was dismissed by sociologists such as Paul Thompson who maintained that the flats 'must be reckoned a social failure (though a sculptural triumph)'. However, their importance in the search for an alternative form of urban housing has been recognized by their listing.

Denys Lasdun & Partners. Housing, Claredale Street, Bethnal Green, London (1959) *Photos: Tom Bell*

Eric Lyons. Parkleys, Ham Common, London (1956)
Photo: Peter Pitt

▶ Founded by Geoffrey Townsend, Lyons' erstwhile partner, who resigned his RIBA membership to become a developer, Span Developments Limited (including the builder/developer, Leslie Bilsby, and with Lyons as its architect) set new standards in speculative housing construction. The company was born of Townsend's and Lyons' conviction that there was a market for modern housing – as opposed to the revival styles normally favoured by speculative builders – if it was well designed and affordable. They were convinced that rather than simply condemning its excesses, architects should re-engage in speculative housing to raise standards and thereby demonstrate their indispensable role in domestic design. Moreover, they felt that architects were in danger of becoming mere technicians and of ceding design control to planning authorities, and that they needed to reassert their status as creative designers. Although undertaken before Span's formation, Parkleys, which was Lyons' and Townsend's first major development and consisted of 160 flats in two-storey terraces and three-storey H-plan blocks, contained all the main features which were to become characteristics of Span's work. These included a carefully crafted layout which eschewed streets in favour of courtyards; landscaping treated as an integral part of the design; low, tile-hung terraces; cross-wall construction; standardization of kitchens, bathrooms and other components to maximize production; and, last but not least, the creation of an association of residents charged with the upkeep of the dwellings' exteriors and communal spaces – an essential component of Lyons' desire to create true community housing.

▶ Lyons articulated Span's design strategy as the use of 'simple crude building elements involving the highly repetitive use of structural elements and equipment and – this is an architectural heresy – involving repetition of similar buildings on *different* sites'. Despite this standardization, essential to keep costs down, Span developments were far from stereotyped. As can be seen in the cluster of schemes at Blackheath, the developments were subtly varied according to the sites and there was an ongoing programme of refinement of detail and experimentation with different housing prototypes. Lyons was concerned to redress what he perceived as the Modern Movement's failure to use exterior space creatively and Span developments were distinguished above all by their landscaping, especially the way in which the communal gardens and spaces, around which the houses and flats were grouped, were sensitively scaled to the buildings themselves thus creating a real sense of enclosure – compare this to much New Town housing lost in an ocean of dead space. Although achieving high densities, Span developments, largely restricted to middle-class London suburbs and hampered by the conservatism of planning authorities and building societies, were criticized as irrelevant to the overall housing problem. Nevertheless they were widely imitated – to the point of cliché as far as the weatherboarding was concerned – and by combining good design with marketability gave fresh impetus to private enterprise housing.

Eric Lyons. The Priory, Blackheath, London (1957)
Photo: Peter Pitt

This terrace of six three-storeyed houses was designed by Stanley Amis and Bill and Gillian Howell for themselves and four other families while they were working in the London County Council Architects Department on Alton West and it continued themes under investigation there. The site had previously been occupied by four Victorian houses, but to keep costs low greater subdivision was necessary and this resulted in a very narrow 12 ft frontage to each house. As this was remarkably similar to the modular dimension employed by Le Corbusier's Unité, Marseilles, which the architects had visited in late 1952, the dimensions of the houses were worked out according to the precepts of *Le Modulor* which Bill Howell also helped to translate. Another Corbusian feature was the use of double-height rooms which afforded fine views over Hampstead Ponds at the rear of the terrace. Ingeniously and compactly planned, each house had subtle variations tailored to differing individual requirements. The houses were also a notable instance of the use of cross-wall construction which facilitated their internal variations.

Stanley Amis and Bill and Gillian Howell. Six houses, South Hill Park, Hampstead, London (1956)
Photo (ext): Eric de Maré
Photo (int): John Pantlin

56   BUILDING A BETTER TOMORROW

The commission to design these speculative flats came through Stirling's friendship with Paul Manousso, whose father, Luke, was a developer intent on proving that 'there is a public who would reject the poor appearance and often low building standards of estate housing offered to them if modern design was available'. This scheme, together with another obtained by Gowan for a house on the Isle of Wight, enabled the two architects to set up private practice together in 1956. Sited on a long narrow strip in the grounds of a Georgian country house, the 30 flats were arranged in three blocks, one of three storeys and two of two storeys. All were characterized by the use of sharply detailed but largely unfinished materials – chiefly brick and concrete but also wood – in a 'cleaned-up' version of Le Corbusier's Maisons Jaoul which Stirling had visited in 1954 and criticized for its 'mannered imperfectionism'. If their plan derived from De Stijl, the scale and general appearance of the flats, with their elevations expressing the structural system, had more clearly English antecedents in anonymous, indigenous structures such as brick kilns and warehouses which Stirling knew from his native Liverpool and wrote about in a 1957 article entitled 'Regionalism in Modern Architecture'. This potent mixture of foreign and vernacular influences was indicative of a more uncompromising approach to architectural design which gained the scheme and the architects international recognition.

Stirling & Gowan. Housing, Ham Common, Richmond, London (1958)
Photos: Colin Westwood

**Peter Womersley. Farnley Hey,
Farnley Tyas (1955)**

▶ Begun in 1952 but not completed until just after the relaxation of building restrictions in 1954, Farnley Hey symbolizes the transition from post-war austerity to a new mood of optimism. Superbly exploiting its dramatic location at the edge of a steep cliff over a densely wooded valley, the house – Womersley's first work – is a good example of the varied influences at play on a young designer in the 1950s. In its organic quality and use of rough stone, both within (as wall finishes) and without (the house stands on a Yorkshire stone plinth), it recalls the work of Frank Lloyd Wright. Similarly its informality of plan and use of different materials to distinguish different zones of the house derive from Le Corbusier. However, there are also English antecedents. The concern to relate the house to its landscape setting was very much in tune with the contemporary revival of picturesque theory, while the extensive use of timber followed on from pre-war works such as Serge Chermayeff's house at Halland (1938) where modernist architects had at last begun to cast off the straitjacket of reinforced concrete and white render to explore the possibilities of a wider range of materials especially brick and wood. An extension, planned from the start, was carried out in 1956 and today the house survives relatively unaltered.

Peter Womersley. Farnley Hey, Farnley Tyas (1955)
Photo: Hugh de Burgh Galwey

In the treatment of its interior space, Farnley Hey typifies the 1950s 'Contemporary' look. The house was designed for Womersley's brother and his wife, one of whose chief requirements was that it should be suitable for large parties and musical entertainments both live and recorded. This together with the smallness of the house – it was only approximately 16,000 sq ft, the maximum permitted at the time – dictated an open plan. Almost the whole of the interior was thus given over to a large double-height living area with different 'rooms' being demarcated not by internal walls or partitions but by changes in floor level, by visual interruptions such as sideboards, music units and structural columns and by the use of different surface textures, and changes in lighting. The illusion of spaciousness was further enhanced by the generous expanse of picture window, the provision of outdoor porches and terraces, and the minimal space devoted to circulation, Womersley maintaining that 'the staircase is as much a piece of furniture as a link between the different levels of the house'. Illustrated and reviewed in *House and Garden*, which thought it 'remarkable for the richness of the materials and the sense of luxury it creates', the house won instant critical acclaim and was highly influential, a mock-up of it even being exhibited in the British Pavilion at the Brussels Expo in 1958.

James Cubitt & Partners.
22 Avenue Road, Leicester
(1954)
Photo: Alfred Cracknell

▶ Designed for a family of five in 1951–2 when building restrictions still applied, this house was ingeniously and compactly planned on American lines to fit its owners' requirements into the maximum permissible floor space of 1,500 sq ft. L-shaped, it was divided into two separate wings, connected only by a kitchen/passage, to allow adults and children to enjoy a degree of independence. The larger adult wing contained the main living room, with south-facing floor-to-ceiling windows, the kitchen, where space was saved by incorporating a Wastemaster rubbish disposal unit into the sink, and the parents' bedroom suite. As the house was actually built after restrictions had been relaxed, richer materials and finishes could be used and these were seen to best effect in a series of specially designed fitted cupboards veneered in various kinds of wood.

Another feature was the underfloor heating. Bearing resemblances to the near-contemporary house Stefan Buzas, a member of the firm, designed for himself at Ham, the Leicester house survives little altered and has been listed Grade II.

▶ Following the success of the Royal Festival Hall, Leslie Martin was invited to design the Nottingham Playhouse, a commission he passed to his colleague, Peter Moro, who, as a result, set up in private practice in 1952. As it transpired, the theatre was not completed until 1964 and in the meantime Moro executed other works such as the Fairlawn Primary School, Lewisham, for the LCC (1957). This brick and timber house, built on the site of a demolished Victorian villa, was designed by Moro for himself and his wife and daughter in the teeth of fierce local opposition to the incursion of Modernism into genteel Blackheath Park. The light interior provided a demonstration of 1950s spatial planning at its most imaginative. Apart from the two guest bedrooms, all the main living and bedroom accommodation was concentrated on the first floor. Interest and variety were lent to the interior by the use of changes in level on both floors – a device extended to the roof where a continuous south-facing clerestory window admitted daylight into the north-facing rooms. A white-painted brick wall broke the interior into two halves and on the first floor separated the bedrooms, bathroom and staircase from a large open-plan area consisting of kitchen, dining room, study and living room, each adroitly demarcated by the split-level plan and half-screens. The painting was by John Tunnard.

Peter Moro. 20 Blackheath Park, London (1958)

HOUSING 61

**Raymond Erith. The Pediment,
Aynho, Northamptonshire
(1957)**

▶ Unfêted for much of his working life, Erith is now acknowledged as Britain's greatest post-war classical architect whose avowed aim was 'to recapture the essential quality of architecture ... which began to disappear sometime during the eighteenth century and which had practically vanished before 1850'. Steeped in the work of Palladio and Alberti, the Architectural Association-trained Erith designed The Pediment in the austere manner of another of his heroes, Sir John Soane, who had worked on the nearby Aynhoe Park. Erith wrote to his client, Miss Watt:

> I think a house with a pediment would fill the bill very well indeed and therefore I am working on a square plan ... The only trouble is that a square house tends to look smaller than it actually is. I do not know if you would mind that; but it would elevate well and have the charm that one occasionally sees in eighteenth-century buildings when they are at once very small and very architectural.

The severe unadorned simplicity of the stone-built Pediment earned Erith the grudging admiration of some of his modernist contemporaries while presaging a more productive phase in his career when, from his office in Dedham, he produced work the best examples of which respected East Anglian traditions. Erith's involvement with The Pediment lasted until his death in 1973, since when his practice has been continued by his partner, Quinlan Terry.

BUILDING A BETTER TOMORROW

**Marshall Sisson. Okeover Hall,
Staffordshire (1960)**
Photo: Edward Leigh

▶ Despite losses during and after the war, the 1950s witnessed an active market in country house building and restoration guided by the writings of Christopher Hussey in *Country Life*, the interior decorations, largely in the eighteenth-century French and English manners, of John Fowler, and the work of architects such as the prolific Claud Phillimore. Okeover is one of the period's best examples, a sensitive solution by Sisson to a house whose straightforward history of ownership – it had been in the same family since Norman times – was matched only by the complexity of its building history. The house as encountered by Sisson was, in Arthur Oswald's phrase, 'a rather pathetic hotch potch'. Remodelled in the eighteenth century by Joseph Sanderson, Okeover had been reduced in size in the early nineteenth century and then enlarged in piecemeal fashion. Beginning in 1953, Sisson reoriented the house, demolished the nineteenth-century additions and restored the 1750 east wing which he cleverly integrated into what was essentially a new house even though it incorporated elements salvaged from the demolitions. In his assured handling of the classical idiom can be discerned Sisson's debt to the American classicist, John Russell Pope, in whose New York office Sisson had worked during his Duveen Fellowship in 1927. Sisson carried out other country house restorations which reflected pre-war works such as Colchester Public Library (1939) rather than the Modernism of Gull Rock, Carlyon Bay (1934).

Selecting fabrics at Heal's (1956)
Photo: John Maltby

**Kitchen for the Gas Council,
Ideal Home Exhibition (1955)**
Photo: John McCann

64 BUILDING A BETTER TOMORROW

Canada Trend House, Ideal Home Exhibition (1957)
Photo: John Maltby

▶ Taste in interior design was shaped by the Ideal Home exhibitions; by magazines such as *House and Garden*, hailed by the *Architects' Journal* as the most influential medium of communication between the architect and his market 'among moderate, middle-class, *Observer*-reading, professional men, with educated wives', *Ideal Home* and *Woman*, which boasted a circulation of 3.5 million and whose editor, Mary Gieve, was a committee member of the influential Council of Industrial Design; and firms such as Heal's. The Canada Trend House, which was intended to demonstrate the benefits of timber construction, was furnished throughout by Heal's whose fabrics were designed by some of the period's most talented designers including Lucienne Day. Such fabrics were an essential ingredient of the 'Contemporary' look lampooned by Michael Flanders who crooned, 'Our search for self-expression leaves us barely time for meals – / One day we're taking Liberty's in, the next we're down at Heal's.' The decade was also marked by major advances in kitchen design sparked initially by the application of wartime mass-production techniques and materials such as aluminium and then by the arrival from America of the concept of the fitted kitchen supplied by specialist firms such as Hygena or, as here, by utility companies like the Gas Council. The fitted kitchen was heavily marketed for its combination of functionality with increasing sophistication and glamour, supposedly in tune with the 'hostess' role of the housewife.

Leslie Gooday & C Wycliffe Noble.
36 West Temple Sheen, London
(1953)
Photo: Peter Pitt

▶ These three architect-designed interiors display many of the fashionable features of the period. Gestetner's flat illustrates the fondness for interior planting derived from Scandinavia, satirized by Osbert Lancaster as 'jungle-jungle' – 'the cacti of the Middle European 'thirties were now outclassed by extraordinary growths, conceived on the Amazon and nurtured in the hothouses of Copenhagen' – and described by Margaret Jones and H F Clark in *Indoor Plants and Gardens* (1952) as 'coinciding with a renewed interest in detail, surfaces and textures, colour relations and landscaping on the part of architects and interior designers'. This concern with surfaces and textures is well shown in Leslie Gooday's own single-storey house, replete with *House and Garden* colours, David Whitehead fabrics, and furniture mostly designed by the architect, where a variety of contrasting materials is employed – rough stonework on the dining area walls, cork-tiled floors, slatted timber on the lounge's exterior wall and buff brickwork for its fireplace. 'Brooycas' is similarly open-plan and its split-level and generous fenestration, which add to the effect of spaciousness, are again characteristic of the period. Equally characteristic are the contrast between the rugged sandstone wall (not seen in the picture) and the richly polished African hardwood floor, the use of boldly coloured wallpaper – bright tomato and white – to emphasize the division between the sitting and dining areas, and Arne Jacobsen's Ant chairs grouped around the table.

BUILDING A BETTER TOMORROW

**Brownrigg & Turner.
'Brooycas', Chantry View
Road, Guildford (1955)**
Photo: Stanley Chapman

**Fritz Gross. Gestetner flat,
12 Charles Street, Mayfair,
London (1950)**
Photo: John Maltby

HOUSING

**Alison and Peter Smithson.
House of the Future, Ideal Home
Exhibition, London (1956)**
Photo: John McCann

In its Jubilee year the *Daily Mail* invited the Smithsons to design a house as it might appear in 1980. Their exhibit consisted of a one-bedroom town house wrapped around a patio garden and moulded in plastic impregnated plaster. This skin, the construction of which borrowed techniques used in motor manufacturing, was made up of a number of units each comprising floor, walls and ceiling treated as a continuous surface. The cave-like interior, which, apart from optional folding doors, had no room divisions, was a hymn to the beneficence of technology. Filled with labour-saving gadgetry such as an electrostatic dust collector, it had few moveable items. All fittings were moulded to the wall surface and at the touch of a control panel part of the living room floor rose up to become a dining or coffee table. Following on from such predecessors as Buckminster Fuller's Dymaxion House (1927), the Smithsons presented their house as a prototype for future living and a demonstration of the benefits which could accrue from architects and manufacturers working closely together. To the public, however, the design was pure science-fiction fantasy, a view reinforced by its male occupant's nylon attire designed by Teddy Tinling to reflect 'a kind of Superman trend to fit in with the Space Age'. In this science-fiction aspect and its embracing of technology the house anticipated the work of Archigram in the 1960s.

Transport

With Sir John Summerson declaring in 1957, 'We still await the moment when British Railways will rise in their majesty and sweep away the junk of a century', the two most salient transportation factors to influence, and indeed consistently outpace, architectural design in the 1950s were the growth in air travel and the doubling of car ownership.

A reappraisal of airport design was necessitated by the technical advances in aviation made during the war which had resulted in larger and faster planes; by the introduction of civil jet aircraft, of which the first, the De Havilland Comet, made its inaugural flight in 1949; and by an increase in passengers attracted by more affordable fares. The heavier aircraft now in use were less susceptible to cross winds but required hardened runways and aprons which could be concentrated in a narrow area. Green field omnidirectional airports such as Croydon where the buildings were clustered around the periphery of the field – what Banham termed the 'yacht-basin' approach to airport design – consequently became obsolescent. The most common type of European airport was that in which, as at Turnhouse, passengers walked from the terminal across the tarmac to planes parked on the apron in front of it. This arrangement became increasingly insupportable, however, as the volume of traffic escalated, causing the distance between terminal and planes to become ever greater. This factor combined with the noise and danger of jet engines dictated the distancing of planes from the terminal building and provision of an enclosed means of conveying passengers between the two.

London Airport (Heathrow) and Gatwick, though built only a few years apart, not only exhibited contrasting styles – Gibberd's Swedish-inspired red brick buildings as opposed to the more rigorous Modernism of Yorke Rosenberg & Mardall – but also represented radically different solutions to this problem. Heathrow was the first of a new breed of airports where the buildings were centrally disposed, in this case in a diamond-shaped wedge formed between the six interlocking runways and thus isolated from the outside world, access to which was through a tunnel. The method of plane parking dictated the terminal's plan. In order to provide direct access to the aircraft stands ranged in a line in front of it, the terminal needed a wide frontage which, however, restricted passenger circulation. By contrast Gatwick's pier system, where passengers left the terminal and walked along the finger to board aircraft parked on either side, allowed the terminal to have a much narrower airside frontage and meant its plan could be greatly simplified since it did not

Robert Paine & Partners. Southern Autos Ltd, Canterbury (1959)
Photo: John Pantlin

have to cater for passengers getting on and off planes. The result was more flexible circulation. Even so, both airports soon required major extensions in a desperate attempt to keep abreast of technological developments and ever expanding airline business.

As Diana Rowntree's condemnation in 1956 of the emergence of the motel which 'has in this country come to the boil with plenty of scum on it' underlined, the car in itself engendered little architecture of significance. Its widespread impact on planning and design nevertheless became increasingly apparent as the decade progressed. Some indication of the car's inexorable progress can be gleaned from a few facts. In 1951 the zebra crossing was introduced; in 1958 parking meters appeared; in the following year the first Mini rolled off the production line and Britain's first motorway, the M1, was opened. This rapid increase in car and commercial vehicle usage, threatening town and country alike and aiding the onward march of 'subtopia', overwhelmed planners and architects. By the time Churchill Gardens and Alton West, for example, were finally completed their seemingly generous provision for car parking proved totally inadequate. Similarly at Harlow initial plans to provide one garage for every ten dwellings soon had to be revised to allow one for every two. Growing awareness of the problem of burgeoning vehicle numbers resulted in the development of a new form of housing layout, which, though variously configured, was generally dubbed 'Radburn' after its 1928 New Jersey pioneer. This abandoned the traditional street frontage and instead concentrated homes in small inward-looking enclaves with service road and cul-de-sacs on one side of the dwellings and access to a network of footpaths on the other. Through traffic was banned. This idea of segregating people and traffic also informed the plans for new town centres such as Coventry and Stevenage and was further developed in the concept of the 'environmental area'. This was a key element in the Ministry of Transport's influential study, headed by Colin Buchanan and published in 1963 as *Traffic in Towns* – official recognition that the motor age had arrived.

Adie Button & Partners with Thomas Bilbow. Stockwell Bus Garage, Lansdowne Way, London (1953)
Photo: John Pantlin

As part of its post-war programme to replace its trams with buses, the London Transport Executive commissioned a series of new garages, the most striking of which was this at Stockwell. Adie Button & Partners, who were responsible for other garages for London Transport including those at Thornton Heath (1953) and Shepherd's Bush (1954), responded to the brief to provide covered, uninterrupted floor space, sufficient to accommodate 200 buses, by designing a dramatic cathedral-like interior, almost 400 ft long, beneath an immense reinforced concrete shell roof. Top lit, the garage was constructed of two-hinged reinforced concrete portal frames spanning 194 ft. These were joined by arched vaults, each spanning 42 ft, which divided the garage into nine bays. Although there was nothing new about this constructional technique – shallow concrete vaulting was, for example, being used contemporaneously but more ambitiously at the Brynmawr Rubber Factory – the garage, in its soaring monumentality, continued the pattern of enlightened architectural patronage which had distinguished London Transport in the 1930s.

Shell garage, Kingston-upon-Thames, London (1957)
Photo: John Maltby

During the 1930s roadside garages with their unsightly signs and apparel of past architectural styles had been the butt of trenchant criticism from bodies such as the Council for the Protection of Rural England. In 1947 the Minister of Transport set up the Waleran Committee to consider the problem of filling station design and although its recommendations were not implemented, it spurred the petrol companies to take a keener interest in the appearance of the outlets which sold their products. From 1951 companies such as Shell-Mex and BP began entering into agreements with individual retailers to stock only their products in return for financial assistance to improve their stations, an initiative that was followed by a programme of limited acquisition of sites by Shell-Mex and BP itself. With this greater company involvement came the economy of scale essential for research and the use of standardized components. In 1952 Shell-Mex and BP sponsored a competition for the design of a modern filling station, two out of its three sections being won by Maxwell Gregory. Building on this, the company architect D A Birchett, then developed a new standard filling station to a modular design with steel framing and curtain walling sufficiently flexible to be adapted to varying sites. First unveiled at Reading in 1955, this standard model drew heavily on the methodology of the Hertfordshire schools and in Hills employed the same manufacturer.

Launched in 1959, the *SS Oriana* maintained the Orient Line's reputation for innovative contemporary ship design established in the 1930s under the aegis of its owner, Colin Anderson. The Design Research Unit, led by Misha Black, was responsible for the ship's badge on its bows and also for coordinating the design of the public rooms. Some of these, such as the first-class lounge and children's playroom, the Unit designed itself while others were entrusted to R D Russell & Partners, who were also responsible for the cabins, and Ward & Austin, whose contribution included the tourist ballroom shown below. Acting as consultant architect was E Brian O'Rorke who had designed some of the best Orient Line interiors of the 1930s such as those for the *RMS Orion* (1935). A feature repeated from the inter-war years was the employment of leading artists, here represented by John Piper, Geoffrey Clarke and Laurence Scarfe. The tourist-class rooms, praised for their 'restrained sophistication', were generally more successful than their first-class counterparts, where the straining after sumptuous effect was too readily apparent. Overall, however, with its generous glazing and light and airy interior the *Oriana* seemed a breath of nautical fresh air compared to other liners of the period which the *Architectural Review* dismissed as comprising 'a bewildering sequence of banalities'.

Design Research Unit, co-ordinating architects.
***SS Oriana* (1959)**
Photos: John Maltby

74   BUILDING A BETTER TOMORROW

**Robert H Matthew.
Turnhouse Airport,
Edinburgh (1956)**
Photo: W J Toomey

Turnhouse began life as an RAF station in 1915 and was converted to civil use to serve as Edinburgh's airport in 1947. Between 1951 and 1955 its passenger numbers more than quadrupled and Matthew was commissioned to design a new terminal building to cope with this increase as well as allow for easy extension at a later date. Matthew's terminal, his first work on his return to Scotland after leaving the LCC, was a characteristically elegant and skilfully planned example of understated Modernism, hailed by fellow architect Michael Laird as 'the matrix of a new Scottish vernacular in the modern movement' but which nonetheless looked as if it had been transported from London's South Bank. The *Architects' Journal* was similarly enthusiastic, praising 'the feeling for wood and the quality of its detailing' which it considered 'reminiscent in elegance and propriety of some of the old railway carriages (first class!)'. Larger than projected increases in passenger traffic caused the terminal to be extended twice, in 1959 and 1965, and also called into question its adoption of open apron aircraft parking. In 1975 a new terminal was designed by Robert Matthew Johnson-Marshall & Partners. The old terminal was finally demolished in 1995.

London Airport opened to civil aviation on 1 January 1946 on the site of a former RAF transport station. Its expansion was rapid and by 1954 it had become the busiest airport in Europe hosting 23 airlines and handling 845,000 passengers a year. In 1950 Gibberd was commissioned by the Minister of Civil Aviation to design the airport's first permanent buildings – the control tower, a passenger handling building and an airline operations building with public facilities (Queen's Building). Housing the most sophisticated equipment in the world at the time which enabled it to control the movements of 50 or more aircraft an hour, the steel-framed control tower bore clear resemblances to Gibberd's The Lawn, Harlow. The tower was 127 ft high with air traffic control services occupying the upper four floors and medical and canteen facilities grouped at its base. Its exterior walls of red brick and artificial stone facing panels were deliberately disposed at varying planes and angles to each other to minimize the interference which large flat surfaces might have caused to radio approach and landing equipment.

Frederick Gibberd. Control Tower, London Airport (1955)
Photo (ext): John Maltby
Photo (int): Colin Westwood

BUILDING A BETTER TOMORROW

Frederick Gibberd. Passenger handling building, London Airport (1955)
Photo: John McCann

▶ Like the control tower, the long, low passenger handling building (now Terminal 2) was constructed on a 12 ft grid. Although it adopted tried and tested methods of passenger circulation, these were on a larger and more complex scale than elsewhere. The ground floor was given over to land arrivals to the terminal via the road tunnel underneath part of the airfield, to baggage handling and to accommodation of technical staff and services. The main passenger facilities were situated on the floor above where a long concourse incorporated at either end ten parallel, self-contained passenger channels which were fully reversible and could thus be used either for incoming or outgoing travellers. The second floor acted as an extension to the concourse with restaurant, bar and viewing facilities and also contained office accommodation for airline workers. A key feature of the terminal was Gibberd's concern that it should be a showcase for British design. Accordingly all the built-in furniture was designed by Gibberd himself, while the movable pieces and furnishings were contributed by, among others, June Lyon, Peggy Angus and Robin Day. The results were sufficiently impressive for the shining new airport to feature as the 'star' of Basil Dearden's portmanteau film, *Out of the Clouds*, made by Ealing Studios in 1954.

Yorke Rosenberg & Mardall. Gatwick Airport (1958)
Photo: Colin Westwood

▶ In 1955 plans were drawn up to extend the existing airport at Gatwick to relieve congestion at Heathrow and provide a possible alternative landing site in bad weather. The resultant new structures, all designed by Yorke Rosenberg & Mardall, comprised a terminal building, control tower, central 'finger' and an operations block. Gatwick was innovatory in two important respects. Firstly, straddling the A23 London to Brighton trunk road and incorporating the adjoining railway station, it was the first airport in the world to integrate road, rail and air transport. Secondly, it was the first airport in Europe to adopt the 'finger' or pier system of aircraft parking, which had already been introduced in the United States. The pier itself was a simple but elegant steel-framed, glass-walled, covered walkway in the Miesian idiom which fully exploited the drama of air travel and provided a sharp contrast to the concrete and brick Brutalist forms of the control tower. Another important feature of the airport's design was its capacity for easy extension either horizontally or vertically. A second phase of construction in 1965 thus saw the main terminal more than double in size and the addition of two more piers, while an office block was added to the roof of the main terminal in 1968.

Yorke Rosenberg & Mardall.
Gatwick Airport (1958)
Photo: Colin Westwood

▶ The terminal was criticized by a doctrinally rigid *Architects' Journal* for its structural dishonesty – 'The building has the look and feel of a steel building and yet in truth it is built of concrete' – and was thus compared unfavourably to Yorke Rosenberg & Mardall's other Gatwick buildings. Even the *Architects' Journal*, however, was forced to concede that the main double-height concourse hall ingeniously combined the myriad different elements essential to the smooth operation of the airport into a coherent whole: 'They have achieved this success by using the space in a big way. By keeping the ceiling clean, exposing the structure boldly and having the same dark floor finish throughout they have made sure that the building by its scale dominates the frippery it contains.' The public areas were notable for an early use by architects YRM of the white glazed tiles which were to become the firm's trademark. Self-cleaning, and facilitating modular and dimensional coordination, these tiles provided the cool, clear, machine finish demanded by the modernist aesthetic.

TRANSPORT

British Railways, Eastern Region Architects Department. Railway Station, Potters Bar (1955)
Photo: John McCann

▶ The architecturally uninspired backdrop against which Celia Johnson and Trevor Howard played out their 'brief encounter' was symptomatic of most railway construction of the period with little new building and maintenance reduced to a minimum. Nationalization in 1948 divided the rail network into six regions each of which had considerable autonomy, an arrangement which militated against an integrated approach to architectural design. Additionally, within each region the architect occupied a lowly position and the sporadic nature of building precluded the establishment of a cohesive programme that could draw on a body of accumulated experience and research. The beginnings of a major modernization programme in the mid-1950s afforded an opportunity to transform this situation and the station at Potters Bar aroused much interest as the first to be completely rebuilt by Eastern Region, the old station having been demolished to accommodate extra tracks. Although its construction helped to underline the important role the architect could play in station design, the new station, influenced by Charles Holden's pre-war London Underground stations, was a modest effort, with extensive use of low-maintenance materials such as tiles, an integrated colour scheme, and a fleeting reminder of the Festival of Britain in the concrete plant holders positioned outside the main entrance. Modernization only got seriously under way in the 1960s and then with often disastrous consequences for the railway heritage.

Worship

Although many uninspiring churches were erected during the post-war period, Kidder Smith's contention in 1961 that 'there are more fine new churches around Basel or Cologne than in the whole of the United Kingdom' was unfair. Sandwiched between the two major ecclesiastical events of the decade – the competition for Coventry Cathedral at its beginning and the spread of the liturgical reform movement towards its end – numerous excellent churches were built in a variety of styles from the neo-Georgian All Saints, Bawdeswell (1955), by James Fletcher Watson, through Sir Giles Gilbert Scott's Gothic Roman Catholic Church of Our Lady of Mount Carmel, Kensington (1959), to Seely & Paget's more original St Luke, Leagrave, Luton (1956).

In 1950 the old masters still held sway. Scott, despite his engineered resignation as architect to Coventry Cathedral, remained active not least with the still unfolding Liverpool Anglican Cathedral; Edward Maufe was likewise occupied with the cathedral at Guildford; Albert Richardson was restoring Wren's bomb-damaged City churches; and Ninian Comper was knighted in 1950. From this traditional stream flowed a number of distinguished new churches which, particularly in the work of Goodhart-Rendel, suggested that, far from drying up, this stream still offered new possibilities for creative interpretation. However, there were signs of change. In 1949 Sir Charles Nicholson, architect to several cathedrals, died and was replaced at Llandaff by George Pace who proved himself one of the period's most distinctively original ecclesiastical architects. In the following year, the new competition conditions for Coventry Cathedral dropped the previous stipulation that the style should be Gothic thereby encouraging a wider range of architects to enter, including the Smithsons whose design took the form of a concrete shell vault. The unveiling of Basil Spence's winning entry in 1951, which disappointed old guard and younger, more radical architects alike, followed by its long gestation until the cathedral's consecration in 1962, focused attention on the future direction of church architecture. From the mid-1950s the debate intensified as, with the easing of restrictions, church building accelerated to meet the need created by bombing, population movements and, especially in the case of the Roman Catholic Church, Irish and Polish immigration.

The church architect's dilemma was how to create a seemingly timeless, spiritually imbued and symbolically meaningful architecture without, in the words of Edward Mills, one of the most

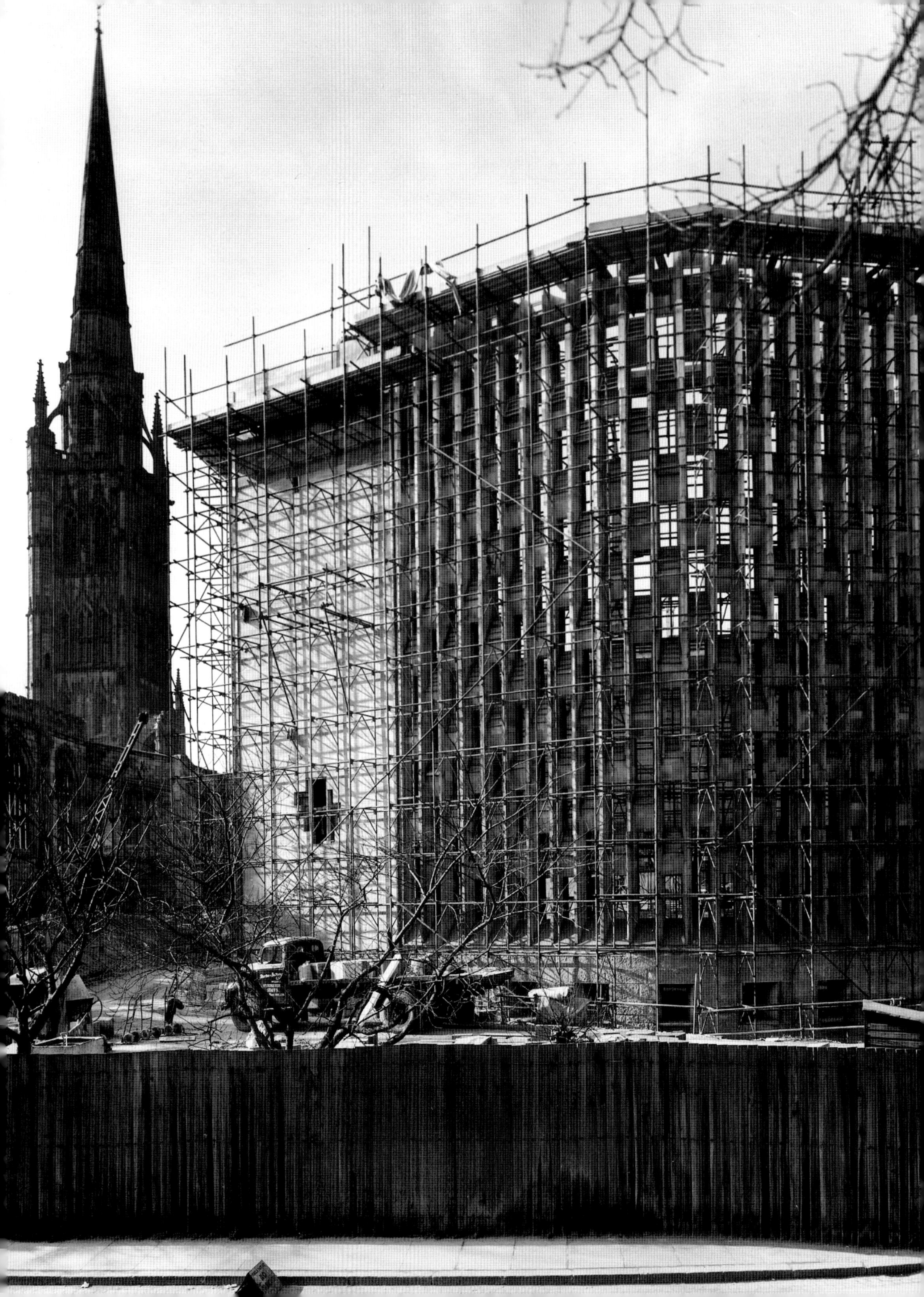

intelligent writers on the subject, 'slavishly copying the past but rather developing a new aesthetic which acknowledges contemporary architectural developments'. The problem was exacerbated by traditionalist clergy and congregations suspicious of any extension of Modernism into the ecclesiastical sphere. This reaction to a modern church captured in Angus Wilson's saga of New Town life, *Late Call* (1964), was not untypical:

> Yet despite the odd metal steeple more like a piece of children's Meccano and the funny slots in the side of the building, it was rather plain inside – spacious and light enough, but more like a lecture hall with unpolished wooden chairs and little tie-on cushion seats covered in jade green American cloth. Apart from a long thin silver crucifix that stood on the altar steps, you'd hardly know it for a church.

While architects like Spence, and, more successfully, Pace, confronted this problem by attempting to synthesize the old with the new, advocates of liturgical reform proposed a more fundamental reassessment of church planning. The movement's clarion call was a challenging article in the *Architectural Review*, April 1958, by Peter Hammond, rector of Bagendon, which was subsequently expanded into his book, *Liturgy and Architecture* (1960). He was scathingly dismissive of much contemporary British ecclesiastical architecture, especially Coventry Cathedral which he maintained 'contributes nothing to the solution of the real problems of church design and perpetuates a conception of a church which owes far more to the romantic movement than to the New Testament or authentic Christian tradition'. Hammond called for churches, in line with continental developments, to dispense with traditional distinctions such as that between nave and sanctuary and to be planned in such a way as to promote worship as a collective experience with increased lay participation. Clergy and architects were also implored to work more closely together as architects and educationalists had done to such effect in Hertfordshire. Hammond's ideas were highly influential and best realized in the work of his fellow members of the New Churches Research Group, Maguire & Murray, whose church at Bow Common Hammond praised as 'the outcome of a systematic application of functional analysis to the problems of church design'. This approach itself, however, quickly came under attack from those such as Mills who saw it as ignoring the vital community and social aspects of religious endeavour.

**Basil Spence. Coventry Cathedral
under construction (1959)**
Photo: Henk Snoek

Cecil C Handisyde and D Rogers Stark. Trinity Congregational Church, Poplar, London (1951)
Photo: John Pantlin

▶ Trinity Church formed part of the Festival of Britain's *Live Architecture Exhibition* which aimed to present a representative cross-section of a modern neighbourhood unit. In accordance with its brief, the church was airy, light and 'Contemporary'. Externally it was distinguished by its sensitive use of materials including the exhibition-prescribed brickwork of yellow London stocks, and by the way its detached bell-tower with etiolated open lantern (which the critic Sherban Cantacuzino reckoned had 'travelled to Poplar from Lombardy via Sweden') acted as a focal point for the composition. The simple interior was notable for its cantilevered galleries which enabled it to accommodate up to 400 people yet also engendered a sense of intimacy when only a small congregation was present. With its auxiliary buildings including assembly hall and clubrooms, the church was designed to cater for a wide range of community activities and in this respect it was highly influential. Cantacuzino remarked, 'At Poplar there is no ritual and the church becomes part of a larger group of buildings that make up a community centre. The spiritual journey from the club-room to the church pew is here a simple matter. . . . We may conclude that contemporary architecture is particularly suited to such simplified forms of the Christian religion as congregationalism.'

**Gillespie Kidd & Coia. St Paul's
Roman Catholic Church,
Glenrothes (1957)**
Photo: W J Toomey

Designed by Isi Metzstein and Andy Macmillan of Gillespie Kidd & Coia, St Paul's in the New Town of Glenrothes marked a significant shift in the firm's work, abandoning the traditional basilican forms of their previous churches for an interior arrangement which reflected the growing influence of the liturgical reform movement. Significantly it was reviewed in the *Architects' Journal* by Robert Maguire, one of the chief proponents of the movement, and as Coia himself wrote, 'Worship is a communal thing ... it requires active participation but to achieve this one must be near enough to understand the Mass'. At Glenrothes the wedge-shaped plan not only allowed all worshippers easily to see the forward altar but also, through its effect of perspective foreshortening, made the sanctuary appear closer to the congregation. The simple white sculptural forms of the minimalist exterior were continued inside where the cleverly arranged distribution of natural light, via the glazed entrance wall for the 'nave' and a concealed light source in the tower for the sanctuary, greatly enhanced the sense of spirituality. Welcomed by the *Architects' Journal* as 'probably the most successful modern church to be built on this side of the English Channel', St Paul's was the first in a series of remarkably inventive churches which established Gillespie Kidd & Coia as the foremost designers of ecclesiastical buildings of the post-war period.

Potter & Hare were among the most imaginative church architects of the period, even managing to win the approbation of the normally censorious Peter Hammond. This church was distinguished by its use of local stone left exposed inside and out and by the curious array of slightly projecting hexagonal windows which were filled with coloured glass and studded into the east wall. The light-filled interior contained interesting works of contemporary art including abstract stained glass by Geoffrey Clarke and a painting by Robert Medley which decorated the underside of the ciborium above the free-standing altar. A projected *Christ in Majesty* sculpted by Sir Jacob Epstein remained unexecuted. For Hammond this was 'one of the most satisfactory buildings for liturgy completed in this country since the war'. It is now listed Grade II.

Potter & Hare. Church of the Ascension, Crownhill, Plymouth (1958)
Photos: Colin Westwood

George Pace. St Michael's Theological College Chapel, Llandaff (1959) *Photo: Stanley Travers*

Pace's productive career, which encompassed both new church building and restoration work, was informed by a concern to fuse the traditional with the modern and thereby create a church architecture expressive of his own age's aspirations. A devout Christian, he was much influenced by the inter-war churches of Dominikus Böhm as well as by the native Arts and Crafts movement as is evidenced by his Scargill Chapel, Kettlewell (1961). His most extraordinary achievement came at the badly bombed Llandaff where his ruthless insertion of a concrete pulpitum with Epstein's *Majestas* across the cathedral's nave, which successfully dissipated its unbecoming parish church atmosphere, was combined with a sensitive restoration of existing work. This nearby chapel was one of his smallest but most perfectly realized modern designs. With its Pennant rubble walls there is little hint of its ecclesiastical function from the outside, but inside Pace memorably captured what he regarded as the essential attributes of church architecture – 'wonder, worship, magic and symbolism'. The interior walls, plastered and painted white, were rounded off, producing a cycloramic effect, while the succession of rectangular windows, punched randomly into the long side wall, recalled Le Corbusier's Nôtre-Dame-du-Haut, Ronchamp (1955) and created a similarly numinous aura. The free-standing altar demonstrated Pace's increasing commitment to liturgical reform and caused the chapel to be reviewed in the *Architects' Journal* alongside St Paul's, Glenrothes – a fitting linking of the two most original post-war ecclesiastical architects.

Basil Spence. St Paul's, Wordsworth Avenue, Ecclesfield, Sheffield (1959)
Photo: Henk Snoek

▶ Spence's triumph in the Coventry Cathedral competition led to a succession of ecclesiastical commissions, mostly in the mushrooming new suburbs of cities such as Coventry and Sheffield. These churches, all built to a modest budget, incorporated ideas Spence had assimilated during two trips abroad – to France and Switzerland in 1956 and to Sweden in the following year – to study ecclesiastical design. They also allowed him to experiment with forms which he could possibly re-use at Coventry Cathedral, the design for which underwent numerous modifications during the decade. St Paul's is a typical example and, in its simplicity and transparency, one of the best. Designed for a congregation of 250, it was built to harmonize with the existing vicarage and hall in an important illustration of Spence's concern that his churches should act as a focus for the community and not be too narrowly concentrated on purely theological functions. It consisted of slightly staggered brick side walls, glazed walls at both ends, and a barrel-vaulted roof which seemed to float on air. The glazed end wall was a motif common to other of Spence's parish churches and recurred in the great west end of Coventry Cathedral. St Paul's was also typical in having a detached campanile, a device inspired by continental precedents, among them St Johannes Church, Basle (1936) by Burckhardt & Egender which was illustrated in Edward Mills' *The Modern Church* (1956) to which Spence contributed the preface.

▶ Mitcham's Methodist church, which replaced the nearby blitzed original church, gave concrete expression to views articulated by Mills in *The Modern Church* (1956) where he wrote, 'A new type of church is envisaged which should not only be the architectural expression of a centre of worship but also provide for the social needs. A church of this character might then, like the medieval church, again become a vital part within the life of the community'. Mills himself was a Methodist and had been nurtured in the tradition of the vast Methodist Central Halls which catered for a wide range of social activities.

To Mills this social component was essential if the church was to roll back the rising tide of secularism. Mitcham, an inexpensive, unassuming church with a folded slab roof supported by a series of reinforced concrete frames devised in conjunction with Ove Arup & Partners, was thus designed for everyday use. Besides the church itself, it comprised a large hall, with stage, for 200 people, three large classrooms and other ancillary facilities. Together with Trinity Congregational Church, Poplar, Mitcham was an important model for the many churches built for multi-functional use during the 1960s and later, their design provoking intense debate as to whether spirituality was being sacrificed on the altar of social relevance.

Edward D Mills. Methodist Church, Cricket Green, Mitcham, London (1959)
Photos: Henk Snoek

Goodhart-Rendel Broadbent & Curtis. Holy Trinity, Dockhead, London (1960)
Photo: Holland & Hannen

▶ Goodhart-Rendel's long career spanned the entire first half of the twentieth century from his earliest works of 1904 to this, one of his last, begun in 1951 but only completed after his death in 1959. During the 1950s Goodhart-Rendel continued to demonstrate his facility in a wide range of styles from the neo-Victorianism of St John the Evangelist, St Leonards-on-Sea (1952), through the rebuilding of 1 Dean Trench Street, London (1954), in the manner of Richard Norman Shaw, to the Greek Revivalism of his, now sadly demolished, extension to offices for N M Rothschild at New Court, London (1954). Holy Trinity was his finest work of the period and a fitting summation to a corpus of building unfortunately overshadowed by the brilliance of his architectural criticism. At Holy Trinity his deep knowledge of architectural history was given full rein in a version of the Romanesque which was indebted to the work of the Victorian ecclesiastical architects he so ceaselessly championed, particularly in its intricately patterned polychromatic brickwork to that of William Butterfield. As D A Reid, one of his assistants at the time, has pointed out, the church also revealed Goodhart-Rendel's strict adherence to a mathematical system of design, the proportions here being based on the equilateral triangle, particularly appropriate for the Trinity and revealed in the hexagonal towers of the west front and the arrangement of the main arches within the concrete barrel-vaulted interior.

Begun in 1958, St Paul's was the flagship church of the liturgical movement, widely publicized and highly influential, and striking evidence that a new generation of church architects was coming to the fore. Its form was influenced not by modern continental precedents but by the teachings of Wittkower, particularly regarding centrally-planned Renaissance churches, which Maguire had imbibed as a student at the Architectural Association. Designed from the altar outwards, St Paul's sought to capture that quality of 'inclusive space' which Maguire believed characterized buildings such as the Pazzi Chapel, Florence and Santa Fosca, Torcello because of their centralizing organization. This, together with the use of light to define space, determined the design of St Paul's in concentric zones with the easily visible altar sited slightly off-centre and surrounded on three sides by modest benches that were portable to allow for flexible use of the internal space. The free-standing sanctuary was simply defined, not by the usual steps and rails, which had the effect of transforming the mass into a dramatic spectacle rather than a shared experience, but by the roof lantern, hanging corona and hard-wearing brick paving designed to withstand kneeling and so an instance of the architects' concern to fuse function and spirituality. Banham wrote that St Paul's would soon be 'denounced as "only a machine for worshipping in", but when it is we shall know that even its detractors have admitted that it has started from essentials, and serves them properly'.

Maguire & Murray. St Paul's, Bow Common, Burdett Road, London (1960)
Photos: Hugh de Burgh Galwey

Leisure and the arts

Paradoxically the 1950s was not only the first television age but also a decade which witnessed an unprecedented rise in participation in leisure pursuits sparked by increasing affluence and the democratization of the weekend. Some of these pursuits, such as skating, were actively promoted as wholesome teenage alternatives to the vicarious pleasures of rock and roll; few demanded architectural solutions and the growth in provision of sporting facilities, for example, only began in the 1960s. Of more immediate architectural concern was the vogue for coffee bars which provided a whiff of exotic cosmopolitanism and gave eclecticism free rein. 'Their slinky, snaky continentalism', reported one observer in 1954,

> is sidling into the British way of life, is infiltrating, outflanking, encountering head-on the bluff, plain Englishry of our Red Lions and White Harts . . . Already they have captured the metropolis; Oxford and Cambridge, inveterate seekers after some thing new, have succumbed to them; their tentacles are round the coasts, their genial lights glow in the murk of industrial towns. Soon we shall have the highest *espresso* on the Westmoreland fells or the North York Moors, the last before Land's End, the oldest in Lincs . . . the Englishman finds himself again in his coffee house; only this time the Englishwoman is with him.

Despite the rising popularity of the domestic hi-fi, television rapidly established itself as the dominant form of home entertainment. In 1952 nearly 1.5 million TV licences were issued but, stimulated partly by the televising of the Coronation in 1953 which was watched by an estimated 20 million viewers, this figure had increased seven-fold by the end of the decade. Ironically, despite the television set's increasing ubiquity as a focal point in the home and a proud symbol of new technology, its styling remained essentially conservative.

Worst affected by this television boom was the cinema which saw an alarming contraction of audiences, from 24.5 million a week in 1954 to 10 million in 1960. With cinemas having been built at such a hectic pace in the 1930s there was now over-capacity and closures inevitably resulted. From a peak of 4,709 cinemas open in Britain in 1946 the number of outlets dwindled to 3,034 by 1960. Many of these were on prime sites and were

Pleasure Gardens, Battersea Park, London (1951)
Photo: John Maltby

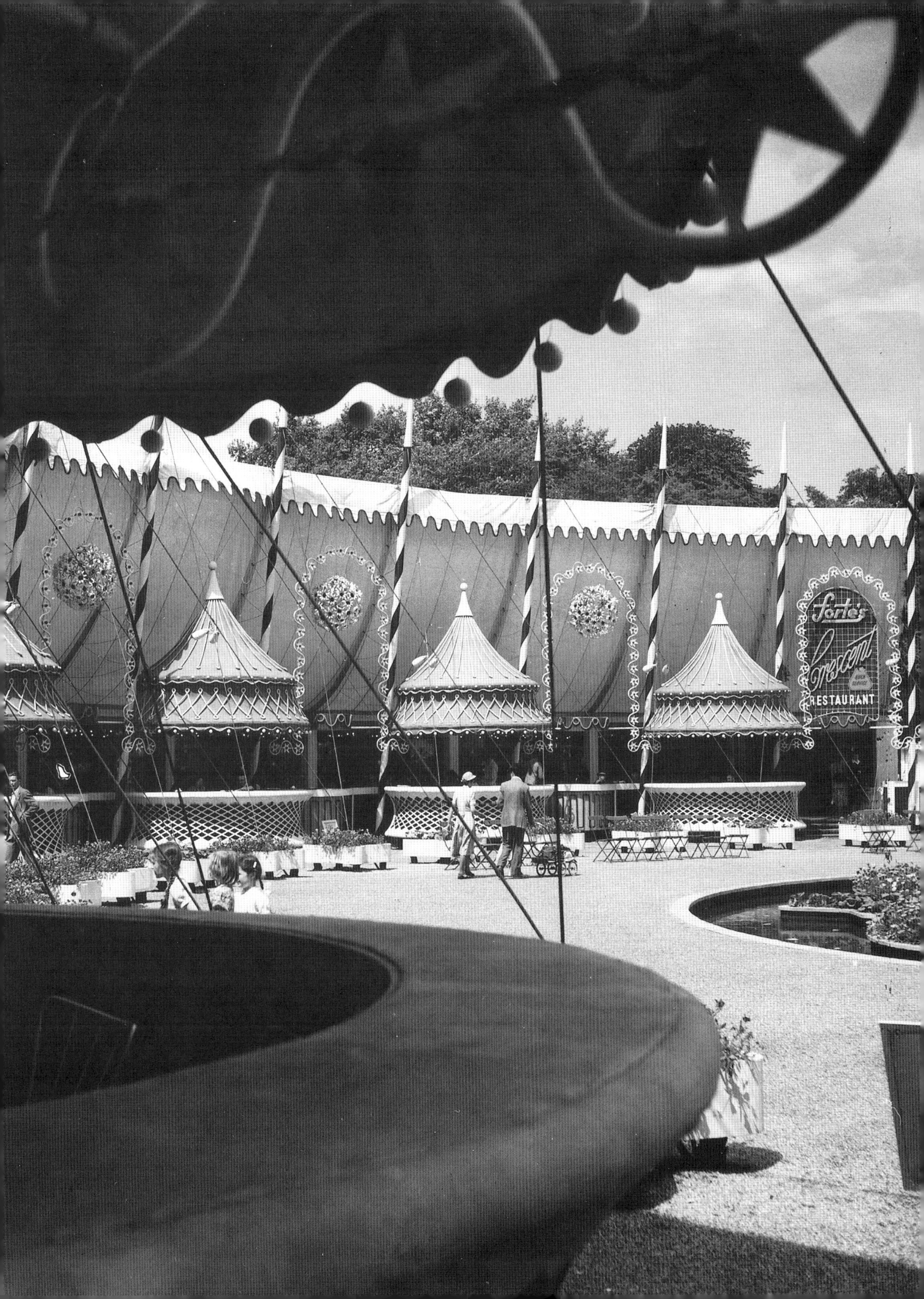
Forte's
Crescent
QUICK SERVICE
RESTAURANT

therefore demolished to make way for profitable redevelopments; others survived by catering to the new craze for bingo. Attempts to lure back the audience with technological innovations such as Cinemascope, introduced in 1954, although initially successful could not halt the overall decline. Among some modest transformations of existing cinemas perhaps the best was H Werner Rosenthal's Cinephone in Birmingham (1956).

Theatre architecture followed a similar pattern. However, the building of the Belgrade towards the end of the decade provoked a clamour for more subsidized provincial theatres which finally bore fruit in the 1960s with the construction of theatres such as Powell & Moya's Chichester Festival Theatre (1962) and Peter Moro's Nottingham Playhouse (1964). The most innovative feature of theatre design in the 1950s was the impetus towards the open platform stage. This was prompted by a combination of economics, in that the open stage could be smaller and eliminated the need for large stores for scenery and workshops; research into Elizabethan and Jacobean stagecraft; and the desire, similar to that in the Church embodied in the liturgical reform movement, to establish a more direct rapport between actors and audience. The open stage was strongly promoted by many actors, theatre designers and historians, such as Richard Leacroft in an article in the *Architectural Review* in 1959, and realized at the Mermaid Theatre in the same year.

Collaboration between architects and artists, which, though imperfectly realized, had been an aim of the Festival of Britain's organizers, was one of the decade's most hotly debated issues. Spence's expressed desire for a marriage between the arts, which in 1959 caused Summerson to worry whether Coventry Cathedral would 'turn out to be a religious building or only the most striking pavilion of religious art of the century', was not shared by a younger generation of architects. Their work at the *This Is Tomorrow* exhibition (1956) generally favoured looser arrangements or even, as in the case of Stirling, a rejection of the idea of collaboration altogether – 'Why clutter up your building with "pieces" of sculpture when the architect can make his medium so exciting that the need for sculpture will be done away with and its very presence nullified.' Similarly the ex-architect turned sculptor, Reg Butler, in a debate at the RIBA in 1958 on 'Architecture and the Other Arts', suggested that architects should simply choose existing pieces by artists they liked for particular spaces – an approach adopted at Harlow.

Lucas Mellinger. Wayang Coffee Lounge, Earl's Court Road, London (1956)
Photo: John Maltby

Michael Naimski and Norman F Plastow. Kon-Tiki Coffee Bar, St Mary Abbots Place, London (1956)
Photo: John Maltby

John & Sylvia Reid. Piazza Coffee Bar, Marylebone High Street, London (1955)
Photo: John McCann

▶ The increasing availability of Italian espresso machines from 1953 occasioned what *Architectural Design* hailed as 'the greatest social revolution since the laundrette'. From their heartlands in Kensington and Chelsea, coffee bars, rejoicing in exotic names such as El Cubano, Gondola and Kon-Tiki, mushroomed in a short-lived outburst of flashy exhibitionism. By 1957 there were over a thousand such bars patronized by a clientele glad to escape the dreary working-class cafe or the pub where perpendicular drinking was still the norm. Some coffee bars were architect-designed and drew on recognizable sources – the Festival of Britain, contemporary exhibition design – but, spurred on by fierce competition, many eschewed tasteful but po-faced architectural involvement in favour of an unabashed theatrical vulgarity reminiscent of the Victorian gin palace. Marghanita Laski described a typical example in the *Architectural Review* in 1955:

> Here are the wooden vertical slats, sometimes up the bar-counter, nearly always facing the box on the floor with the green fleshy plants inside. There are those same little taper-leg wicker-seated backless stools – fortunate to be female and get the banquette. And here are the strings of garlic, the periodicals on bamboo racks, the elliptical mock-Picasso dishes, smaller for ashtrays, larger for marrows and gourds; here are the thick glass coffee-cups on the bare inorganic table-tops, the trolley of rich squashy pastries, and there, overhead, the rectangular Something hanging from the ceiling.

Robert H Matthew, J Leslie Martin, Peter Moro, Edwin Williams of London County Council Architects Department. Royal Festival Hall, South Bank, London (1951) *Photo: Colin Westwood*

▶ The only permanent legacy of the Festival of Britain's South Bank complex, the Royal Festival Hall, has proved one of the country's best and most-loved post-war buildings. That this is so is a tribute to its young, relatively inexperienced, design team who had to work at great speed against a backdrop of severe materials' shortages and bad weather. The hall is important, therefore, not just for its design qualities and its status as Britain's first major public building to be designed wholly in a modern idiom, but also for its production process which placed a new emphasis on teamwork and a more technocratic approach to building. Design work began in 1948 and continued as building progressed to fulfil a brief which called for a large concert hall for 3,000 people with a smaller twin (soon abandoned) together with restaurant, meeting rooms and exhibition gallery. The hall was thus envisaged not just as a concert space but as a social centre, and the problem was to accommodate all these functions on a restricted site. Martin's solution was ingeniously to raise the auditorium on a series of circular, reinforced concrete columns, leaving the foyers free to sweep underneath, and so create a dramatic interplay between the auditorium's solid mass and the light, transparent treatment of the surrounding elements. This was the 'solid egg in the transparent box' which gave the hall its remarkable sense of spatial dynamism and its ability to appear at once monumental yet informal.

Robert H Matthew, J Leslie Martin, Peter Moro, Edwin Williams of London County Council Architects Department. Royal Festival Hall, South Bank, London (1951)
Photo: John Pantlin

The hall is notable throughout for its carefully considered detailing masterminded by Moro with the assistance of designers such as Robin Day who was responsible for the seating. The underlying rationale of Martin's design was emphasized by differing decorative treatments, the dark Derbyshire marble of the auditorium's outer walls, for example, being set off against the cool, bright colours of the circulation areas. These were in turn contrasted with the rich warm hues inside the auditorium. The shoebox shape of the well-lit auditorium was determined by acoustical requirements worked out after extensive scientific testing by Hope Bagenal with Bill Allen and P H Parkin of the Building Research Station. The cantilevered boxes, reminiscent of the balconies at Highpoint I (1935) by Tecton, for whom Moro had briefly worked, were disparagingly compared to drawers hurriedly pulled out in a burglary, but did fulfil an acoustical function by breaking up the walls' flat planes. The acoustics were generally judged good if rather dry. Less good was the paucity of backstage accommodation, scheduled for completion in 1953, but only eventually provided during a major and insensitive remodelling in the 1960s which also saw the frontage recased and extended towards the river. Recent alterations have attempted to undo some of the damage caused to the original conception, but the status of the hall as an icon of post-war idealism and civic service remains unchallenged.

Arthur G Ling,
City Architect and
Planning Officer.
**Belgrade Theatre,
Coventry (1958)**
Photo (ext): Colin Westwood
Photo (int): John McCann

▶ The fact that the Belgrade Theatre was built at all was in many respects of greater significance than its architectural merit. Named in commemoration of a gift of beech wood from Yugoslavia, the Belgrade was one of the few new theatres built after the war in Britain where, in the face of stiff competition from cinema and television, the more general trend was one of closure and demolition. As its first new civic building, the theatre was also an important element, both practically and symbolically, in Coventry's post-war resurgence. Although it was begun in 1956, the year in which John Osborne's *Look Back in Anger* was helping to revolutionize British theatre, the Belgrade afforded no similarly radical architectural parallel. The long glazed frontage and 'drawers pulled out' boxes declared it the progeny of the Royal Festival Hall while its stage was of the conventional proscenium type. As the *Architects' Journal* lamented, 'We still await the unusual and unlikely combination of a theatrical producer client with vision, an architect with vision and a banker with vision'.

▶ The reinforced concrete framed annexe was built to accommodate the Old Vic's scenery workshops, wardrobe stores and administrative offices. A particular difficulty was to incorporate the 30 ft high mechanically operated paint frame on which canvases were prepared. This was sited on the second floor and the finished canvases were then lowered through a 50 ft well to ground-floor level for despatch to the theatre. As there was no precedent for such a building type with a complex internal arrangement, the tightly planned design frankly reflected the varied activities carried on inside. Similarly, as the walls and floor would inevitably be defaced by the type of work undertaken, the brick and rough-shuttered concrete used in the structure were left in their natural state to form the walls while tile and granolithic were chosen for the floors so they would be hard-wearing and easy to clean. In its bold use of exposed materials and honest expression of its structure, the annexe was an important early example of New Brutalism and signalled a shift in the firm's work, largely inspired by Tom Ellis who had joined it in 1947, towards a more Corbusian aesthetic. The firm itself was an important training ground for many prominent practitioners, among whom in the 1950s were Stirling, Gowan, Alan Colquhoun and John Miller.

Lyons Israel & Ellis. Old Vic Theatre Annexe, The Cut, London (1958)
Photos: Hugh de Burgh Galwey

**Devereux & Davies. Mermaid
Theatre, Puddle Dock, London
(1959)**
Photo: Colin Westwood

▶ Conceived by the actor Bernard Miles and his wife, Josephine Wilson, the Mermaid was London's first new theatre for 25 years and the first in the City for 250 years. Unusually it was financed by public subscription with building work progressing as funds became available. The need to keep costs to a minimum resulted in a theatre which was pared down to essentials with the walls of the existing bombed warehouse on the site levelled off and spanned by a reinforced concrete barrel-vaulted roof to form the auditorium. Cost considerations together with a desire to see a more intimate relationship between actors and audience resulted in an open stage, an arrangement strongly favoured by Miles himself whose idea, according to the *Architects' Journal*, 'has been to admit that theatre can't compete with the cinema or TV in realistic presentation and to play on the almost ritual communication between players and audience that can only be achieved in live theatre and to conjure up ideas and emotions and not a mere mechanical illusion'. The seating for 500 was thus arranged in a single, sharply banked tier before the low stage which had no picture frame, curtain, proscenium opening or orchestra pit – the first time this form of open stage had been adopted in a major modern English theatre. The theatre was later remodelled by Richard Seifert & Partners.

An exhibition exploring the relationship between art and architecture was first proposed by Paule Vézelay, the London representative of *Groupe Espace*. Disagreements, however, saw the exhibition largely organized by Theo Crosby, who was a close associate of the Independent Group, an informal gathering of iconoclastic young artists, architects and critics which was based around the Institute of Contemporary Arts and first met in 1952. Twelve groups, each nominally comprising a painter, sculptor and architect, submitted exhibits. Although these included Constructivist works which aimed to bring 'sculpture and architecture together in a genuine synthesis', the more symbolic treatments of the only two exhibits wholly contributed by Independent Group members attracted most attention, while also revealing the Group's internal divisions. Group Two's exhibit, characterized by Hamilton as 'a kind of fun house of all the multifarious intrusion of the mass media into our lives' reflected the Group's obsession with American consumerism, technology and popular culture and together with Hamilton's celebrated poster, *Just What Is It That Makes Today's Homes So Different, So Appealing?*, helped launch British pop art. In contrast, Group 6 exhibited a wooden pavilion with a translucent corrugated plastic roof surrounded by a sand-floored patio. Symbolizing the human need for space, shelter and privacy, this was simply left for the artists to fill with 'as found' and other objects – an informal collaboration described by the Smithsons as 'the "dressing" of a building, its place, by the "art of inhabitation"'.

This Is Tomorrow **exhibition, Whitechapel Art Gallery, London, 1956**

Group Two (Richard Hamilton, John McHale, John Voelcker)

Group Six, *The Patio and Pavilion* **(Nigel Henderson, Eduardo Paolozzi, Alison and Peter Smithson)**
Photos: John Maltby

Gordon Cullen. Mural, Westville Road Primary School, Hammersmith, London (1951) (architect, Ernö Goldfinger)
Photo: Colin Westwood

Henry Moore. *Family Group*, Barclay School, Stevenage (1950) (architects, Yorke Rosenberg & Mardall)

Barbara Hepworth. *Contrapuntal Forms*, Harlow
Photo (1959): John McCann

▶ Schools provided the most receptive outlets for art, especially murals which were most readily appreciated by the children. In Hertfordshire the incorporation of art was actively pursued under the direction of Newsom who was instrumental in acquiring Henry Moore's *Family Group* for Barclay School, the entrance hall of which was also graced by Kenneth Rowntree's mural. However, Moore's angry protest at the siting of his work revealed his hostility to the presumed subservience of sculpture to architecture. Undeterred, Newsom supported Easton & Robertson's commissioning of *The Oracle* from the controversial sculptor, Reg Butler, for Hatfield Technical College (1953). Matching Hertfordshire in its drive to embrace art was the LCC which in 1956 established a £20,000 annual fund to procure art for its schools and housing estates, a good example being Pasmore's relief and mobile for Moro's Fairlawn School. Perhaps the greatest commitment to arts patronage, however, came at Harlow where works by Moore and Hepworth were acquired, such as the latter's *Contrapuntal Forms*, previously displayed at the Festival of Britain. Harlow's policy of mostly purchasing existing works rather than commissioning new ones – Ralph Brown's *Meat Porters*, Market Square (1956–60) being a notable exception – and using art in Gibberd's words to 'add additional and visual diversity to the urban spaces in which it was set', was in contrast to that of Peterlee where Pasmore was invited to play a more integral design role. Both approaches, however, signalled a new appreciation and renaissance of public art.

102   BUILDING A BETTER TOMORROW

Commerce and industry

Wartime improvements in industrial production filtered through into new factory design of the 1950s, Edward Mills noting the key changes in his *The Modern Factory* (1951): 'To-day much greater interest is taken in the layout of plant, production efficiency and improved working conditions. Large unobstructed floor areas are now commonly demanded, together with improved artificial and natural lighting, heating, air-conditioning and insulation.' The decade produced one outstanding example of industrial architecture in the Brynmawr Rubber Factory and one consistently innovative firm in the field in Farmer & Dark. Although considered by Mills to be rigid and over-designed, Brynmawr constituted a worthy radical successor to Owen Williams' magisterial Boots Factory, Beeston (1932). Rejecting the traditional solution of prestige architect-designed offices at the front masking a production shed for workers behind, Brynmawr was an exercise in social democracy attempting to break down distinctions between white- and blue-collar workers through an integrated design. The significant engineering input at Brynmawr was also a feature of the work of Farmer & Dark, who produced a series of progressive designs including, in addition to Marchwood Power Station, buildings for Loewy Engineering, Poole (1953), and for Bowater at Northfleet (1957–60). On a smaller scale the decade also saw the introduction of the flatted factory, the first example being designed for Birmingham Corporation by Philip Skelcher & Partners in 1957.

The major 1950s trends in retailing were the growth in self-service shops, the first having appeared in 1948; the spread of multiple shops and chain stores; and the development of the shopping centre. With odd exceptions such as shoe shops like that designed in Oxford Street for Bata by Bronek Katz & R Vaughan (1956), most large chains were architecturally banal. More creative expression was evident in the design of smaller shops and showrooms from the restrained elegance of Alan Irvine's Torrington Furs, New Bond Street, London (1955), to the theatricality of Imhof. The most significant innovation was the increasing adoption of the picture window which, by rendering the shop front transparent, placed greater emphasis on the display within thereby restricting the architect's role to the design of a suitable backdrop to the merchandise. In travel bureaux and showrooms where there were no goods to sell a more wholly architectural solution resulted. Writing in 1957 Herbert Tayler emphasized the important role of shop design:

James Cubitt & Partners. Finmar showrooms, Kingly Street, London (1953)

It is the modern shop interior which has suddenly made the whole modern style in architecture real to the public. . . . if 'Contemporary' has arrived in the suburbs, in the provinces, and in the council houses, it is through the décor of shops, not the early modern domestic interiors . . . Because everyone looks at shops, the interior, suddenly revealed, could not fail to be the most influential piece of architecture for twenty years – a popular free exhibition of modern design, and the public lapped it up.

The rise of the property developer in the latter half of the decade saw a rash of office building designed to achieve the maximum space to let. This was accompanied by a discernible trend away from the tall office block orientated around a dank interior courtyard and presenting a vertiginous frontage to the street, to a different type of tower or slab block set back from or sited at right angles to it. This design enabled the offices to face outwards with correspondingly better lighting. While welcoming this transformation, *The Times* noted in 1957, 'The change we have to accept as the price of this improvement in planning is the disintegration of the street facade; densely built up city centres are being transformed from a number of unbroken corridor streets with an even skyline into a number of masses rising into the sky, leaving the street to represent simply the line of traffic on the ground.' These increasingly tall blocks were much influenced by two New York prototypes – Skidmore Owings & Merrill's Lever House (1952) and Mies van der Rohe's Seagram Building (1958).

In the case of the smaller office building the problem was often one of harmonization with its neighbours. Two contrasting approaches are represented by Goldfinger's Albemarle Street and Gollins Melvin Ward & Partners' Electrin House. Of the two, Goldfinger's was more sophisticated but Electrin House, through its curtain walling, spurned by Goldfinger as producing 'buildings with masks like those stockings burglars use', proved more of a harbinger of things to come. Allowing dry construction and rapid erection and betokening a modern machine aesthetic, curtain walling was to become an all too familiar part of the urban scene, capable occasionally of elegant refinement but often marked by diagrammatic monotony.

Architects' Co-operative Partnership. Factory for Brynmawr Rubber Company, Brynmawr (1951)
Photo: H Tempest

▶ The Brynmawr Rubber Factory was one of the most remarkable post-war buildings, a striking mix of architectural ingenuity, innovative engineering, enlightened patronage and social vision fashioned during the darkest days of Britain's post-war crisis when headlines screeched, 'Shiver with Shinwell and starve with Strachey'. The factory, conceived to aid regeneration in the economically devastated region of South Wales by using local labour and coal, was the brainchild of James Forrester, later 5th Earl of Verulam, and director of Enfield Cables of which the rubber company was a subsidiary. With the approval of the official client, Wales and Monmouthshire Industrial Estates Ltd, Forrester entrusted the design to four members of the as yet untried Architects' Co-operative Partnership some of whom were already in his employ. To ACP, founded in 1939 by eleven radical young architects fresh out of the Architectural Association, Brynmawr offered an unrivalled opportunity to put their ideas into practice. Chief among these was a belief in architecture as a social science responsive to the needs not just of particular clients but of society as a whole and a consequent emphasis on team working, especially close collaboration with engineers on all aspects of the design. Taking as its model the Barcelona-based GATEPAC, ACP above all eschewed what one of its members, Anthony Cox, contemptuously dismissed as the 'prima donna' approach to architecture.

Architects' Co-operative Partnership. Factory for Brynmawr Rubber Company, Brynmawr (1951)

▶ The collaboration between architects and engineers is shown above all in the design of the imposing main production area which was located at the heart of the factory. Here the requirement was for an unbroken floor area to permit maximum flexibility of production. With steel scarce, the engineer, Ove Arup, and his partner, Richard Jenkins, devised a system which pushed the possibilities of concrete shell construction to their limits. Resembling giant eggshells and arranged in three rectangular blocks, nine thin concrete domes each 85 ft × 62 ft – the largest of their kind in the world – spanned the production area's 77,000 sq ft of floor space, a design solution given added significance by the way it allowed the integration of mechanical and electrical services. As important as this engineering triumph was the social vision underlying the factory's design which envisaged it as a blueprint for a new form of industrial democracy. Thus there was a common entrance for management and workers and the canteen and excellent welfare facilities were similarly shared. The factory, however, proved an economic and social failure. In 1954 it was sold to Dunlop who added a separate office block and so reversed the democratic principles on which the design philosophy had been based. Today, derelict and with its future uncertain, Brynmawr remains a poignantly evocative symbol of the dissolution of the post-war consensus and the withering of the hopes for a more egalitarian Britain which underpinned it.

▶ This unusual factory comprised two separate but interconnected buildings – a processing block and a warehouse – which served the differing functions associated with seed storage. These buildings also needed to be kept apart to prevent the possible spread of fire, the previous warehouse having burnt down. Although both were planned on a 5 ft grid, were similarly clad, and made forceful use of colour contrasts, the architects deliberately created a tension between the two by emphasizing in their differing designs and structures the active nature of the processing block as opposed to the static character of the warehouse. When seed arrived it was hoisted to the top of the five-storey processing block and then dropped down, floor by floor, to be dried and cleaned en route. The vertical nature of this processing precluded the fireproofing of the floors – hence the need for separation – and dictated a steel frame. The warehouse, by contrast, was a rectangular three-storey concrete block with each floor unbroken and fireproofed and all vertical circulation kept to the outside. The floor slabs were also projected beyond the screen wall to act as a firebreak. The scheme, which the architects described as 'lovely engineering' and which was influenced by the Smithsons' school at Hunstanton, was awarded an RIBA Bronze Medal in 1957.

Chamberlin Powell & Bon.
Seed factory for Cooper Taber & Co, Station Road, Witham
(1956) *Photos: John Maltby*

COMMERCE AND INDUSTRY

Egon Riss. Rothes Colliery, East Fife Coalfield, Thornton (1957)
Photo: Hugh de Burgh Galwey

▶ Rothes Colliery, now demolished, was part of an ambitious expansion programme initiated by the Scottish Division of the National Coal Board after the industry's nationalization in 1948. Riss, an Austrian émigré who had arrived in England in 1938 and subsequently joined the Miners' Welfare Architects Department, moved to Scotland in 1949. There, in his capacity as Divisional Architect for Production, he designed a number of collieries including Killoch (1953) and Monktonhall (1965). Although at Rothes the pithead baths and canteen were designed by the Welfare Architect, Donald Jack, Riss still achieved a remarkable degree of integration, planning the buildings in a logical disposition to create efficient circulation of men and equipment. This design was a significant improvement over that of many other collieries where production suffered because miners often had to collect their tools, lamps, etc. from a variety of scattered buildings. Architecturally the colliery took its cue from the nearby Glenrothes New Town then being developed to house the miners. Most dramatic of all were the monumental reinforced concrete winding towers, the functional severity of which imparted an austere beauty. Riss' ability to combine successfully architecture and engineering prompted Patrick Nuttgens to hail his collieries as 'one of Scotland's most significant contributions to the story of modern architecture' in the post-war era.

Ove Arup & Partners; associated architect Philip Dowson. Research and production buildings and offices for CIBA (ARC) Ltd, Duxford (1958) *Photo: Colin Westwood*

▶ This factory complex attracted critical attention as 'the product of a structural engineer having an associated architect within the walls of his office', thus raising the thorny issue of whether the architect should maintain his independence or whether private offices should become interdisciplinary. The architect in question was Philip Dowson who had joined Arup on leaving the Architectural Association in 1952 – a sign of the growing recognition of Arup's incalculable contribution to modern architecture. This commission was therefore an important stage in the evolution of Arup Associates, a partnership of architects and engineers, officially established in 1963. Adopting a similar rationale to the factory at Witham, the complex comprised various buildings of differing, functionally determined structural techniques. The photograph shows the reinforced concrete framed process block clad almost entirely in patent glazing which was projected from the structure on metal ladders. As this block was used for the manufacture of inflammable epoxy resins, it was sited at some distance from the other buildings, its refulgent translucence contrasting with the research laboratory (in the background of the photograph) described by the *Architects' Journal* as 'Mondrianesque, forthright and definitive'. The article concluded, 'The basic structural decisions have been the entire *raison d'être* for the aesthetic expression, with a complete absence of tricks of camouflage or clichés. On the face of it these buildings are solid evidence in favour of architects and engineers working on adjacent drawing boards.'

Farmer & Dark. Marchwood Power Station, Marchwood (1959)
Photo: J W Kitchenham

▶ During the 1950s the combination of technical advances in electricity production and the advent of much more powerful generating stations occasioned a fundamental reassessment of power station design. One of the first results of this rethink was Marchwood, the crisp, clean lines of which represented a radical departure from the massive monumentality of the traditional 'brick cathedral' approach to power station architecture epitomized by Sir Giles Gilbert Scott's Battersea (1934) and Bankside, London, then still under construction. Like the Brynmawr Rubber Factory, Marchwood essayed a new fusion of architecture and engineering resulting in a design which, rather than being shamefacedly disguised in a fancy dress of brick cladding, was more frankly expressive of its purpose, fully justifying Pevsner's assessment of the station as 'one of the best pieces of post-war industrial architecture in Britain'. Working in close cooperation with the consulting engineers, Sir William Halcrow & Partners, Farmer & Dark devised several different cladding systems to meet civil defence requirements and the varying needs of different parts of the station. The most intriguing of these encased the magnificent turbine hall in aluminium sheeting which acted like a giant Venetian blind and at night ensured the station was dramatically illuminated over Southampton Water. Commissioned in 1951, Marchwood began generating in 1955 but only went into full production in 1959.

James Cubitt & Partners with Sergei Kadleigh. South African Tourist Centre, 70 Piccadilly, London (1951)
Photo: Alfred Cracknell

▶ During the early 1950s building restrictions dictated that most of the shops built were either travel bureaux or premises for export firms. One particularly striking example was the South African Tourist Centre, described by the *Architectural Review* as 'the most advanced and imaginative frontless shop yet attempted in London'. Following on from Maxwell Fry's Electricity Showroom, Regent Street (1938), the centre exemplified the quickening post-war trend towards the wholly glazed shop frontage with often frameless window and door and no stallboard. The architects drew the eyes of passers-by inexorably into the centre by slightly recessing the frameless plate glass window thereby allowing the flanking walls, one covered in Tinos marble slabs, the other by a large map of South Africa, to continue uninterrupted from exterior to interior.

This 'invisible' frontage meant the interior itself became the display. Here, in a travel bureau, this was less of a problem than in a shop where the goods were constantly changing and the architect therefore had less control. The centre's interior, praised for its 'kaleidoscope patterns', was marked by its studied scaling, use of strong colours and exotic plants to suggest South Africa, and its undulating sycamore-slatted ceiling. James Cubitt & Partners were also responsible for other travel agencies for Quantas, next door at number 69, and Iceland (1952) before increasingly working abroad.

**Tayler & Green. Showroom for
A Imhof Ltd, New Oxford
Street, London (1954)**
Photo: Tayler & Green

▶ For Imhof, Tayler & Green created one of the finest shop interiors of the period opening up Robert Atkinson's existing 1929 steel-framed building in a richly illusionistic display of mirrors, lighting and decorative effects which reflected their interest in theatre and Tayler's sensitivity to the problems posed by contemporary shop design. These he revealed in an article published in the *Architectural Review* in 1957, where he argued that the post-war development of the open shop front, of which Imhof was an outstanding example, had made the role of the shop architect akin to that of the theatrical producer: 'Mere window dressing had now to become overall dressing, with all the discipline, as well as the gaiety, which that naval term implies or which the rise of a curtain in the theatre implies.' Replying to criticism of the shop by Bryan and Norman Westwood, themselves writers on shop architecture, Tayler & Green wrote in the *Architect & Building News* in 1954, 'The intricacy of a gin-palace, the confusion of a successful party, neo-Oxford-Street-baroque: this is the mood we tried to create, by request and by instinct, in Imhof's Shop, and we have, it appears, shocked Messrs. Westwood. Of course, it's vulgar, of course it's overdone, of course it is not serious modern architecture and sales, we are told, have gone up marvellously as a result.'

Dennis Lennon. Showrooms for Vono Ltd, Grosvenor Street, London (1954)
Photo: John McCann

This scheme involved the conversion of existing premises into showrooms and offices for the bed manufacturers, Vono Limited. The pavement side of the showroom's recessed plate glass window was dominated by a sculpture in copper, concrete and iron by Lynn Chadwick entitled *Chrysalis* and appropriately depicting rest. Another decorative feature was a large photomural – a device popular in commercial architecture of the period – illustrating London and the Thames c1860 which ran from the pavement along one side of the window into the interior. These decorative elements were effectively contrasted with the rigidly geometric interior which was lit from a succession of large plaster domes. The showroom was an early work by Dennis Lennon, who, by the end of the decade, had established his firm as one of the leading specialists in interior decoration, especially of shops and hotels – a status which helped it to win the commission for the interior design of the *QE2* (1965–9). Other clients during the 1950s included Jaeger, for whom Lennon designed a shop in Oxford (1954), and Yardleys.

**Denys Lasdun. Peter Robinson
Store, Strand, London (1959)**
Photo: Henk Snoek

Built on the site of the old Tivoli Theatre this was Lasdun's only commercial building and a fine contribution to London's street architecture. Although five-storeys high the store was given a pronounced horizontal emphasis by the reinforced concrete screen wall, clad in reconstructed Portland stone, which ran the entire length of the first floor and was continued round the corner. Above, a deeply recessed clerestory window provided light to the showroom within and separated the cubic form of the screen wall from the sales floor and offices on the three upper storeys. All these latter were clad entirely in pressed bronze sections – the first time such extensive use of bronze cladding had been made in a post-war building.

The aura of cool detachment the Strand facade exuded was continued inside the store where subdued backgrounds by the Design Research Unit allowed the merchandise to be displayed to best effect. The building subsequently became the London headquarters of the New South Wales Government.

Arthur G Ling, City Architect and Planning Officer.
Shopping precinct, Coventry
Photo (1960): John McCann

▶ The post-war reconstruction of Coventry, which attracted keen interest both at home and abroad, ostensibly had its origins in the terrible destruction wrought by the bombing raids of November 1940. However, the unprecedented rise in the city's population, brought about by the workforce requirements of the rapidly expanding car and munitions industries, had already put severe pressure on the city's infrastructure. On his appointment as City Architect in 1938, this pressing situation spurred Donald Gibson, to consider improvements, even though planning officially came under the aegis of the city engineer, E H Ford. In the wake of the bombing both Gibson and Ford were invited to submit proposals for the redevelopment of the central areas. Whereas Ford envisaged merely improving the existing medieval street pattern, Gibson proposed a much more radical replanning with controlled zoning of different activities including a pedestrianized shopping precinct axially aligned in Beaux-Arts manner with the spire of the old cathedral. Unlike Warsaw and other European cities whose rebuilding looked to recreate their past, with the acceptance of Gibson's proposals Coventry embraced wholesale redevelopment on contemporary lines. After many vicissitudes and some alterations Gibson's plan was realized by his successor, Arthur Ling. The shopping precinct arranged on two levels, though supposedly inspired by the Rows at Chester, clearly owed much to the layout of the Festival of Britain and, though architecturally uninspired, proved popular.

Leonard G Vincent, Chief Architect, Stevenage Development Corporation. Town centre, Stevenage (1959) *Photo: John Maltby*

▶ Christened 'Silkingrad' after the Minister of Town and Country Planning by those opposed to its expansion, Stevenage became the first designated New Town in 1946. Although architecturally largely undistinguished, it achieved international fame for its shopping centre, the first fully pedestrianized example of its type in the country and a prototype for many to follow. Mindful of the sharp increase in car usage, the segregation of pedestrians and traffic had been advocated by planners for numerous towns and cities such as Coventry (as early as 1941), Harlow and Crawley, but these proposals met fierce resistance from local businesses and were only partially implemented. At Stevenage it was the local residents who demanded pedestrianization and the first stage of the precinct, designed to cater for 80,000 potential users and consisting of a mixture of small shops, multiple stores, offices, flats and maisonettes, was opened in 1959. A major influence on the centre, discernible especially in the canopies connecting the shops near first-floor level and acting both as a unifying element for the architecture and as a protection for shoppers, was Rotterdam's Lijnbaan, a single pedestrianized street built as part of that city's post-war reconstruction. The centre also graphically illustrated the dominant effect of the car on town planning in its provision of two extendible car parks for the large number of visitors it was expected to attract from a wide radius.

Although he was forced to fend off stiff competition from standfitters, who had traditionally built exhibition stands, and newly emergent professional exhibition designers such as James Gardner and Beverly Pick, to the work-starved architect exhibition design offered, in Neville Conder's words, 'something to make honest money while waiting to do the big thing.' One such was Fritz Gross who designed a string of stands for firms such as the British Tyre and Rubber Company, Monsanto Chemicals and Ferranti which attracted international attention. In addition to his domestic practice, Leslie Gooday also established a reputation for exhibition work, the aerial display he designed for the Hulton's Boys and Girls Exhibition at Olympia reflecting the contemporary obsession with space travel and the exploits of the *Eagle* comic's hero, Dan Dare, while also illustrating the opportunity stand design afforded for fantasy and experimentation. Many of the best stands of the period were for firms such as ICI which introduced new ranges of synthetic products such as Perspex and Terylene and were consequently keen to project an image of scientific modernity. As the decade progressed firms combining the skills of architect and designer such as Neville Ward and Frank Austin and, most notably, the Design Research Unit, whose work encompassed industrial design and graphics as well as architecture, came increasingly to the fore.

Fritz Gross. Ferranti exhibition stand, Radio Show, Earl's Court, London (1952)
Photo: John Maltby

Leslie Gooday. Hulton's Boys & Girls Exhibition, Olympia, London (1956)
Photo: Carl Sutton

ICI exhibition stand, Brussels World's Fair (1958)
Photo: John Maltby

**Michael Rosenauer (architect), Sir Hugh Casson (coordinating designer for interiors) with Misha Black.
Time-Life International, New Bond Street, London (1953)**
Photo: David Potts

What has become known as the Time-Life Building was in fact designed by Michael Rosenauer for Pearl Assurance who let most of the building to Time-Life International as its European headquarters. In 1951, in cooperation with Rosenauer, Time-Life appointed Festival of Britain stalwarts, Sir Hugh Casson and Misha Black, to lead a formidable group of artists and designers, including Henry Moore, Robin Day, R D Russell and R Y Goodden, in transforming the interior into a showcase for contemporary British design and craftsmanship.

The photograph shows the reception room, with curtains by F H K Henrion and an iron sculpture by Geoffrey Clarke, looking towards a mural by Ben Nicholson – these latter among the many art works controversially removed by Time-Life in 1992. As each designer was free to interpret the client's brief as he saw fit, the results, though opulent and imaginative, were criticized for their lack of coherence. Betraying his frustration with the constraints of austerity, Casson retorted that 'most architects have had enough of purges' and what was 'wrong with bursting out a bit'. The critic, Ian McCallum, while finding it 'a little humiliating' that it had taken American money to create the interior, hoped that it would presage a new era in office design by weaning big business off 'monumental Queen Anne and Bankers' Georgian' – a hope which remained largely unrealized.

**Ernö Goldfinger. Offices for
Carr & Co, Cranmore Boulevard,
Shirley, Birmingham (1956)**
Photo: Hugh de Burgh Galwey

This design for a prestige office block adjacent to the company's paper factory contains many elements typical of Goldfinger's work: it is planned on his usual 2 ft 9 in grid; the main elevation clearly expresses its reinforced concrete frame; photobolic screens are used to deflect daylight deep into the interior; and a spiral staircase at its north end provides the single sinuous relief to an otherwise austerely classical, compact facade. The main offices are on the first and second storeys which Goldfinger designed as open floors to allow easy accommodation of changing subdivisions in line with his view that there were three components of office design, 'the permanent structure, the much less permanent services and an even more fleeting component, the human requirements'. These offices are raised on pilotis over the ground-floor reception area, encased in plate glass, allowing, Goldfinger wrote to his client, 'that spatial organisation which you may have admired on the Continent'. Also characteristic of Goldfinger is the assured handling of materials, the concrete on the exterior in a variety of finishes – exposed aggregate, bush hammered and *béton brut* – contrasted with the use of more lavish finishes within such as the marble flooring in the reception area. Carr & Co served as a prototype for later Goldfinger office buildings such as Alexander Fleming House, London (1963).

COMMERCE AND INDUSTRY

**Ernö Goldfinger.
45–46 Albemarle Street,
London (1958)**
Photo: Colin Westwood

▶ This scheme comprised two buildings which, with the cooperation of the owners, Goldfinger was able to integrate into a single design described by *The Times* as 'repay[ing] close study as an exact modern equivalent of eighteenth-century street architecture'. In this respect it parallels Goldfinger's 1–3 Willow Road, Hampstead, London (1939), where he breathed fresh life into the Georgian terrace by reinterpreting it in a wholly modern idiom. The proportions of the Albemarle Street facade, which revealed Goldfinger's debt to his mentor, Auguste Perret, were calculated according to the Golden Section, reflecting Goldfinger's emphasis on symmetry – a legacy of his Beaux-Arts training – and also the post-war revival in interest in proportional systems generally. The design was attacked by both conservative critics and modernists like Jim Richards, who was aggrieved at the way the boxed-out bays stretched across both buildings thus breaking with modernist orthodoxy that the elevation should reflect the interior planning. Lewis Mumford, writing in the *New Yorker*, however, was nearer the mark, 'Here is a building that has not merely learned the lessons of modern form but has learned them thoroughly enough to feel free to learn, too – from the eighteenth century and the Regency – how to create a lively facade for a street that must be modernized. Here the past has been neither externally imitated nor crassly rejected but inwardly absorbed and recreated.'

**David du Rieu Aberdeen.
Trades Union Congress,
Great Russell Street,
London (1957)**
Photo: Colin Westwood

▶ Aberdeen won the competition to design a new headquarters and memorial building for the TUC in 1948 and worked up more detailed designs shortly thereafter which overcame the difficulties of a restricted site and adroitly incorporated the array of diverse facilities the TUC required – conference centre, training college, library, council suite, offices, etc. A building licence was not obtained until 1953, however, and the headquarters was only completed – remarkably with the original designs unaltered – in 1957. This long gestation accounts for the building's slightly anachronistic feel. Conceived before Le Corbusier's conversion to *béton brut*, it harks back to his earlier projects such as the competition entry for the Centrosoyuz building, Moscow (1929), the influence of which is clearly discernible in the Great Russell Street facade. The Bainbridge Street frontage also combines elements derived from the same period – balconies from the Dessau Bauhaus (1926) and the curved, prow-like glass frontage at the junction with Dyott Street from Hans Scharoun. What distinguishes the building, however, and what certainly would not have been possible in 1948, is the superb quality of the detailing and finishes, most of them in traditional materials such as mosaic, bronze, marble and hardwood, which are used to luxurious effect and reflect the meticulous attention Aberdeen gave to even the smallest item.

**David du Rieu Aberdeen.
Trades Union Congress,
Great Russell Street, London
(1957)**
Photo: Colin Westwood

With its reticent exterior and muted colours within, the TUC building looked to two major sculptural works, both only unveiled some time after it was opened, to provide dramatic impact. The bronze by Bernard Meadows outside the main entrance proved disappointing. Inside, however, in the central courtyard around which the building is massed, was Sir Jacob Epstein's memorial to trade unionists killed in the two world wars, carved *in situ* from a huge granite block and one of his last and greatest works. Set on a plinth clad in Roman stone and against a massive 'cliff' of Genoa green marble (since replaced), the memorial depicts a woman holding her dead son in a composition which was shocking in the angry intensity of its indictment of war. Although provoking the usual controversy which surrounded his work, the collaboration between Epstein and Aberdeen was one of the decade's most successful and fruitful instances of artist and architect working together and helped to seal the building's reputation as one of the finest of the period – a judgement endorsed by the Department of the Environment in 1988 when it made it one of the first post-war buildings to be listed.

▶ Built as a speculative office development, Electrin House represented, in the words of *Architectural Design*, 'the first completely uncompromising use of the curtain wall techniques to be built in London'. The curtain wall, which here was designed on a 2 ft 10 in module and comprised extruded aluminium sections with black steel windows and infill panels of blue-grey Vitroslab, was welcomed by critics as an 'anonymous piece of machine architecture' which re-imported from the United States, in particular from Lever House, New York and the Alcoa Building, Pittsburgh (1953), 'the hard-won lessons of functionalism' which had been 'lost in the '30s in the attempt to found a style'. Gollins Melvin Ward, who used 'current techniques with precision and without remorse' and were responsible for a similar curtain-walled building opposite at 118–126 New Cavendish Street, had thus helped to put architecture back on the right track. The *Architects' Journal* went even further, noting the way the office block harmonized with its brick and stucco neighbours and maintained the scale and character of the neighbourhood, and positing through curtain walling the birth of a 'new urban vernacular' – 'It could well be the twentieth-century equivalent of the Georgian facade – an ideal means of creating or preserving unity in the street scene.'

Gollins Melvin Ward & Partners. Electrin House, 93–97 New Cavendish Street, London (1957)
Photo: Colin Westwood

Gollins Melvin Ward & Partners. Castrol House, Marylebone Road, London (1959)
Photo: Henk Snoek

▶ Begun in 1955 to designs initially prepared by Casson & Conder, Castrol House reflected the changing face of London and of British architecture generally at the end of the decade. A speculative development by Hammerson in an area previously considered too far from the City to earn a sufficient return, it highlighted the increasing involvement of property developers in reshaping the urban fabric. Together with Sir Basil Spence's near contemporary Thorn House, Castrol House was also one of the first buildings to take advantage of the relaxation of height restrictions of 100 ft in the capital, in the process sparking fierce debate about the appropriateness of tall buildings. Most importantly of all, taking its inspiration from Lever House, New York, Castrol House introduced into Britain the tower on the podium formula which was to be widely adopted but seldom to the refined effect of airy lightness achieved here. Finally, continuing the experiments made by Gollins Melvin Ward at Cavendish Street, the building was notable for its curtain walling, in this case aluminium cladding with black anodized mullions in the podium contrasted with blue-green glass spandrels in the tower. As the tower cladding came in units complete with windows, half-mullions and transoms which could be factory assembled, fixing on site was kept to a minimum. The office block is now being converted into flats.

Bibliography

My main source of information has been the journals of the period. The following is a list of the secondary sources which have proved most useful.

Allan, John, *Berthold Lubetkin: Architecture and the Tradition of Progress* (RIBA Publications: London, 1992).

Archer, Lucy, *Raymond Erith: Architect* (Cygnet Press: Burford, 1985).

Architecture Today: an Exhibition Arranged Jointly by the Arts Council and the Royal Institute of British Architects (London, 1961).

Banham, Mary and Bevis Hillier (eds), *A Tonic to the Nation: the Festival of Britain 1951* (Thames & Hudson: London, 1976).

Banham, Reyner, *New Brutalism* (Architectural Press: London, 1966).

Banham, Reyner, 'Revenge of the Picturesque: English Architectural Polemics, 1945–1965', in John Summerson (ed), *Concerning Architecture: Essays on Architectural Writers and Writing Presented to Nikolaus Pevsner* (Allen Lane/The Penguin Press: London, 1968).

Campbell, Louise, *Coventry Cathedral: Art and Architecture in Post-War Britain* (Clarendon Press: Oxford, 1996).

Cantacuzino, Sherban, *Howell Killick Partridge & Amis: Architecture* (Lund Humphries: London, 1981).

Curtis, William J R, *Denys Lasdun: Architecture, City, Landscape* (Phaidon: London, 1994).

Dannatt, Trevor, *Modern Architecture in Britain* (Batsford: London, 1959).

Elwall, Robert, *Ernö Goldfinger* (Academy Editions: London, 1996).

Esher, Lionel, *A Broken Wave: the Rebuilding of England 1940–1980* (Allen Lane: London, 1981).

Forsyth, Alan and David Gray (eds), *Lyons Israel Ellis Gray: Buildings and Projects 1932–1983* (Architectural Association: London, 1988).

Glendinning, Miles (ed), *Rebuilding Scotland: the Postwar Vision 1945–1975* (Tuckwell Press: East Linton, 1997).

Glendinning, Miles and Stefan Muthesius, *Tower Block: Modern Public Housing in England, Scotland, Wales, and Northern Ireland* (Yale University Press: New Haven & London, 1994).

Hammond, Peter, *Liturgy and Architecture* (Barrie & Rockliff: London, 1960).

Harwood, Elain, 'Liturgy and Architecture: the Development of the Centralised Eucharistic Space', *Twentieth Century Architecture*, no 3, 1998, pp50–74.

Harwood, Elain and Alan Powers, *Tayler and Green, Architects 1928–1973: the Spirit of Place in Modern Housing* (Prince of Wales's Institute of Architecture: London, 1998).

Jackson, Lesley, *The New Look: Design in the Fifties* (Thames & Hudson: New York, 1991).

Jackson, Lesley, *'Contemporary': Architecture and Interiors of the 1950s* (Phaidon: London, 1994).

Jones, Margaret E and H F Clark, *Indoor Plants and Gardens* (Architectural Press: London, 1952).

Kidder Smith, G E, *The New Architecture of Europe* (Penguin Books: Harmondsworth, 1961).

Landau, Royston, 'The History of Modern Architecture that Still Needs to Be Written', *AA Files*, no 21, Spring 1991, pp49–54.

Landau, Royston, *New Directions in British Architecture* (Studio Vista: London, 1968).

MacDonald, Sally, *Putting on the Style: Setting Up Home in the 1950s* (Geffrye Museum: London, 1990).

McKean, John, *Royal Festival Hall: London County Council, Leslie Martin and Peter Moro* (Phaidon: London, 1992).

Maguire, Robert, 'Annual Lecture 1995: Continuity and Modernity in the Holy Place', *Architectural History*, vol 39, 1996, pp1–18.

Marriott, Oliver, *The Property Boom* (Hamish Hamilton: London, 1967).

Mills, Edward D, *The Modern Church* (Architectural Press: London, 1956).

Mills, Edward D, *The Modern Factory* (Architectural Press: London, 1951).

Neumann, Eva-Marie, 'Architectural Proportion in Britain 1945–1957', *Architectural History*, vol 39, 1996, pp197–221.

Pace, Peter G, *The Architecture of George Pace 1915–75* (Batsford: London, 1990).

Penn, Colin, *House of To-day: a Practical Guide* (Batsford: London, 1954).

Pidgeon, Monica and Theo Crosby (eds), *An Anthology of Houses* (Batsford: London, 1960).

Powers, Alan, *In the Line of Development: FRS Yorke, E Rosenberg and CS Mardall to YRM, 1930–1992* (RIBA Heinz Gallery: London, 1992).

Robbins, David (ed), *The Independent Group: Postwar Britain and the Aesthetics of Plenty* (MIT Press: Cambridge, Mass. & London, 1990).

Robinson, John Martin, *The Latest Country Houses* (Bodley Head: London, 1984).

Rosenberg, Eugene, *Architect's Choice: Art in Architecture in Great Britain since 1945* (Thames & Hudson: London, 1992).

Russell, Barry, *Building Systems, Industrialization, and Architecture* (John Wiley: London, 1981).

Saint, Andrew, *Towards a Social Architecture: the Role of School-Building in Post-War England* (Yale University Press: New Haven & London, 1987).

Stamp, Gavin, 'Acts of Faith: George Pace, Llandaff and Post-War Architecture', *Apollo*, vol 136, September 1992, pp173–80.

Thompson, Paul, *Architecture: Art or Social Service?* (Fabian Society: London, 1963).

Yorke, F R S and Penelope Whiting, *The New Small House* (Architectural Press: London, 1953).

Index

A Imhof Ltd *112*
Abercrombie, Sir Patrick 10, 14, 15, 48
Aberdeen, David du Rieu *121*, *122*
Acoustics 17, 97
Adamsez 34
Adie Button & Partners *72*
Aircraft 28, 69
Airports 69, 71, 75–79
Alberti, Leon Battista 62
Allen, William 97
Allford, David 21
Alloway, Lawrence 12
Aluminium 27, 28, 65, 110, 123, 124
Amis, Stanley 20, *56*
Amusement parks 93
Anderson, Sir Colin 74
Angus, Peggy 77
Archigram 68
Architects' Co-operative Partnership *72*, 103, *105*, *106*, 110 See also Architects' Co-Partnership
Architects' Co-Partnership 17, 18 See also Architects' Co-operative Partnership
Architects' Journal 9
Architectural Association 62, 91, 105, 109
Architectural Design 19
Architectural Review 9, 12, 14, 15, 18, 19, 24
Architecture & engineering 17, 44, 103, 105, 106, 107, 108, 109, 110
Art in relation to architecture 29, 34, 45, 86, 87, 94, 102, 113, 118, 122
Arup, Sir Ove 17, 44, 106
Arup Associates 109
Aslin, C H 9, 17, 30
Asplund, Gunnar 14, 25
Athens Charter 19
Atkinson, Robert 112
Austin, Frank 117
Aycliffe (Durham) 15
Aynho (Northants)
  Aynhoe Park 62
  The Pediment *62*

Bagenal, Hope 97
Banham, Reyner 18–20, 38, 69, 91
Barr, A W Cleeve 13, 48
Basel (Switzerland) 81
  St Johannes 88
Bawdeswell (Norfolk)
  All Saints 81
Beeston (Notts)
  Boots Factory 103
Bell, Tom 53
Belper (Derbyshire)
  Secondary school 39
Bergh Apton (Norfolk)
  Church Road housing *14*
Bickerdike, John *42*
Bilbow, Thomas *72*
Bilsby, Leslie 54
Birchett, D A 73
Birmingham (W Midlands)
  Carr & Co, Cranmore Boulevard, Shirley *119*
  Cinephone 94
  Flatted factory 103
Black, Misha 26, 28, 29, 74, *118*
Böhm, Dominikus 87
Bon, Christoph 52
Boyne, Colin 19
Brett, Lionel See Esher, Lionel Brett (Lord Esher)
Brickwork 15, 37, 44, 47, 49, 57, 61, 66, 69, 76, 84, 88, 90, 91, 99, 110
Bristol 22
British Railways, Eastern Region Architects Department *80*
British Tyre & Rubber Company 117
Bronek Katz & R Vaughan 103
Bronze 114
Brown, Ralph 102
Brownrigg & Turner 66, *67*
Brussels (Belgium)
  British Industries Pavilion, World's Fair, 1958 25
  British Pavilion, World's Fair, 1958 59
  ICI exhibition stand, World's Fair, 1958 *117*
  World's Fair, 1958 25
Brynmawr (Blaenau Gwent)
  Brynmawr Rubber Factory *72*, 103, *105*, *106*, 110
Buchanan, Sir Colin 71
Building Reseach Station 16–17, 97
  Architectural Physics Division 17
Building restrictions 9, 10, 12, 17, 42, 58, 60, 111, 121
Burckhardt & Egender 88
Bus garages 72
Butler, Reg 94, 102
Butterfield, William 90
Buzas, Stefan 60

Cadbury-Brown, H T 43
Cambridge (Cambridgeshire)
  House, Clarkson Road 21
Camouflage Development & Training Centre 13
Cantacuzino, Sherban 47, 84
Canterbury (Kent)
  Southern Autos Ltd *70*
Carlyon Bay (Cornwall)
  Gull Rock 63
Carr & Co *119*
Cars & traffic planning 69, 71, 73, 116 See also Roads, road transport
Casson, Sir Hugh 18, 25, *118*
Casson & Conder 124
Chadwick, Lynn 29, 113
Chamberlin, Peter 52
Chamberlin Powell & Bon 11,12, *16*, 21, *52*, *107*, 109
Chandigarh (India) 18
Chapman, Stanley 67
Chermayeff, Serge 58
Cheshunt (Herts)
  Burleigh School *33*, *34*
Chester (Cheshire)
  The Rows 115
Chicago (Il)
  Minerals & Metals Research Building, Illinois Institute of Technology 37
Chichester (W Sussex)
  Chichester Festival Theatre 94
Churches, chapels 22, 81–91
  liturgical reform 83, 85, 87, 91, 94
  multi-functional 84, 89
CIAM See Congrès Internationaux d'Architecture Moderne
CIBA (ARC) Ltd 109
Cinemas 92, 94, 98, 100
Civic Trust 22
Cladding 110, 114
Clark, H F 12, 66
Clarke, Geoffrey 74, 86, 118
Clarke Hall, Denis 37
CLASP 32, 39
Coates, Wells Wintemute 18
Coffee bars 92, 94, 95
Coia, Jack 85
Colchester (Essex)
  Colchester Public Library 63
Collieries 108
Cologne (Germany) 81
Colour 13, 34, 42, 44, 47, 49, 66, 80, 111
Colquhoun, Alan 99

Comper, Sir Ninian 81
Concert halls 96, 97
Concrete construction 27, 33, 36, 39, 50, 57, 72, 78, 79, 89, 90, 96, 99, 100, 107, 108, 109, 114, 119
  cross-wall construction 17, 44, 54, 56
  Freyssinet system 36
  shell construction 72, 81, 106
Conder, Neville 117
Congrès Internationaux d'Architecture Moderne 19
Connell, Amyas 18
Connell Ward & Lucas 18
Consortium of Local Authorities Special Programme See CLASP
'Contemporary' style 11, 18, 29, 59, 65, 84, 104
Cooper Taber & Co 107
Corby (Northamptonshire) 15
Cotton, Jack 9, 22
Council for the Protection of Rural England 73
Council of Industrial Design 65
Country houses 22, 62, 63
County of London Plan 10, 44, 48
Coventry (W Midlands) 26, 39, 71, 88, 115, 116
  Belgrade Theatre 94, *98*
  Coventry Cathedral 18, 19, 81, *82*, 83, 88, 94
  Shopping precinct *115*
Cox, Anthony 105
Cox, Oliver 13, 48
Cracknell, Alfred 60, 111
Crawley (W Sussex) 43, 116
Crosby, Theo 19, 101
Crowley, Mary See Medd, Mary
Croxley Green (Herts)
  Little Green Lanes Junior School 13
Cubitt, James 10
Cullen, Gordon 12, 15, 22, 47, *102*
Cumbernauld (N Lanarkshire) 15
Curtain walling 22, 73, 104, 123, 124
Cwmbran (Torfaen) 15

Daily Mail 68
Dannatt, Trevor *2*, 21
Darbourne & Darke 46
Day, Lucienne 65
Day, Robin 77, 97, 118
De Maré, Eric 20, 56
De Stijl 57
Dearden, Basil 77
Denys Lasdun & Partners 21, *53* See also Lasdun, Sir Denys
Design Research Unit 29, *74*, 114, 117
Dessau (Germany)
  Bauhaus 121
Devereux & Davies 94, *100*
District heating 46
Dowson, Sir Philip 109
Drew, Dame Jane 10, *28*
Dubuffet, Jean 20
Dunlop 106
Duxford (Cambs)
  Research & production buildings & offices for CIBA (ARC) Ltd 109
Dykes Bower, Stephen 22

East Africa 18
East Kilbride (S Lanarkshire) 15
Easton & Robertson 102
Eastwick-Field, John 16
Edinburgh
  Avisfield, Cramond 21
  Turnhouse Airport 69, *75*
Eliot, T S 40
Ellis, Tom 99
Enfield Cables 105
Epstein, Sir Jacob 86, 87, 122
Erith, Raymond 22, *62*
Esher, Lionel Brett (Lord Esher) 18
Essendon (Herts)
  Primary school *33*, *34*

Factories 103, 105–107, 109, 119
  flatted factories 103
Farmer & Dark 17, 103, *110*
Farnley Tyas (W Yorks)
  Farnley Hey 21, *58*, *59*
Ferranti 117
Finsbury Metropolitan Borough Council 45
Flanders, Michael 65
Florence (Italy)
  Pazzi Chapel 91
Ford, E H 115
Forrester, James 105
Forshaw, J H 10, 14, 48
Foster, Norman (Lord Foster of Thames Bank) 13
Fowler, John 63
Freeman Fox & Partners 27
Fry, E Maxwell 10, 18, *28*, 50, 111
Fry Drew & Partners 28
Fuller, Richard Buckminster 68
Furniture & fittings 9, 21, 29, 59, 60, 65, 66, 68, 77

Galbraith, J K 24
Galwey, Hugh de Burgh 50, 59, 91, 99, 108, 119
Garchey waste disposal system 44
Gardner, James 117
Gas Council *64*, 65
GATEPAC 105
Gatwick Airport (W Sussex) 69, 71, *78*, 79
Gibberd, Sir Frederick 9, 15, 18, 41, *43*, 49, 69, 71, 76, 77, 102
Gibson, Alexander 29
Gibson, Sir Donald 12, 16, 24, 39, 115
Gieve, Mary 65
Gillespie Kidd & Coia *85*, 87
Glasgow 22
Glenrothes (Fife) 15, 108
  St Paul's Roman Catholic Church *85*, 87
Goldfinger, Ernö 18, 21, 22, 36, *102*, 104, *119*, *120*
Gollins Melvin Ward & Partners 21, 24, 40, 104, *123*, *124*
Gooday, Leslie 66, 117
Goodden, R Y *28*, 118
Goodhart-Rendel, Harry Stuart 12, 18, 22, 81, 90
Goodhart-Rendel Broadbent & Curtis 90
Gowan, James 57, 99
Great Britain. Ministry of Education 13, 16, 17, 32, 36
  Architects' & Building Branch 32, *35*, 39
Great Britain. Ministry of Information 25
Great Britain. Ministry of Town & Country Planning 12
Great Britain. Ministry of Transport 71, 73
Green, Absalom *45*
Gregory, Maxwell 73
Gropius, Walter 13, 30, 50
Gross, Fritz 66, 67, 117
Groupe Espace 101
Guildford (Surrey)
  'Brooycas', Chantry View Road 66, 67
  Guildford Cathedral 81
Gwynne, Patrick *19*, 21

Hales (Norfolk)
  1–16 The Boltons *47*
Halland (E Sussex)
  Bentley Wood 58
Hamilton, Richard *101*
Hammerson, Lew 9
Hammerson Properties Ltd 124
Hammond, Peter 83, 86
Handisyde, Cecil C 16, *84*, 89
Harlow (Essex) 15, 18, 71, 94, 116
  Contrapuntal Forms 102
  The Lawn 41, *43*, 49, 76
  Mark Hall North *43*
Hatfield (Herts)
  Technical College 102
Hawksmoor, Nicholas 20

Heal's 64, 65
Henderson, Judith 19
Henderson, Nigel 19, *101*
Henrion, F H K 118
Hepworth, Dame Barbara *102*
Hertfordshire County Architects
    Department 13, 15, 16, *33*, *34*
    schools 9, 10, 13, 17, 18, 19, 30, 32,
        33, 34, 35, 36, 37, 38, 39, 51,
        73, 102
High Sunderland (Scottish Borders)
    Bernat Klein residence 21
Hill, Oliver 18
Hills & Company 33, 35, 73
Hitchcock, Henry-Russell 17
Holden, Charles 80
Holford, Sir William 22
Holland, James 11
Holland & Hannen 90
HORSA 30
House & Garden 65, 66
Houses, housing 11, 12, 14, 15, 21, 22,
    41–68, 71, 102
    balconies, balcony access 44, 45, 46
    cluster blocks 21, 53
    density 15, 22, 41–42, 43, 46, 50, 54
    maisonettes 41, 46, 49, 50, 52, 53
    mixed development 14, 15, 41, 48,
        49, 50, 51
    open-planning 42, 59, 61, 64, 66
    point blocks 41, 43, 49, 50, 53
    prefabs *See* Prefabrication, system
        building
    slab blocks 41, 43, 46, 50, 53
    speculative housing 42, 54, 55, 57
    terraced housing 15, 43, 47, 49, 56
Howell, Bill 20, 50, *56*
Howell, Gillian 20, *56*
Hunstanton (Norfolk)
    Secondary school, King's Lynn Road
        18–19, *37*, *38*, 47, 107
Hussey, Christopher 63
Hutting Operation for Raising the School
    Leaving Age *See* HORSA
Hygena 65

ICI *117*
Ideal Home 64, 65
Independent Group 19, 101
Institute of Contemporary Arts 101
Interior design, interior decoration 59,
    60, 61, 64–68, 74, 77, 91, 95,
    111, 112, 113, 118, 119
Irvine, Alan 103

Jack, Donald 108
Jacobsen, Arne 66
Jaeger 113
James Cubitt & Partners 60, *104*, *111*
Jenkins, Richard 106
John Brockhouse & Company 39
Johnson, Francis 22
Johnson, Philip 18, 38
Johnson-Marshall, Sir Stirrat 13, 16, 17,
    30, 32
Jones, Margaret 66

Kadleigh, Sergei *111*
Kettlewell (N Yorks)
    Scargill Chapel 87
Kidder Smith, George 21, 51, 81
Killoch (Ayrshire)
    Colliery 108
Kingston School of Art 52
Kitchenham, J W 110
Kitchens 64, 65

Lacey, Dan 39
Laird, Michael 75
Lancaster, Sir Osbert 66
Landscape & architecture 11–12, 15, 26,
    47, 48, 49, 51, 54, 55, 58 *See
    also* Plants, planting
Lang, Susan 12

Lasdun, Sir Denys 21, *114 See also* Denys
    Lasdun & Partners
Laski, Marghanita 95
Le Corbusier 20, 21, 50, 53, 56, 57, 58,
    87, 99, 121
Leacroft, Richard 94
Leavesden (Herts)
    Primary school *33*
Leicester
    House, 22 Avenue Road 60
Leigh, Edward 63
Lennon, Dennis 113
Lewis, H J Whitfield 14
Libraries 40
Ling, Arthur G 94, *98*, *115*
Liverpool (Merseyside)
    Anglican Cathedral 81
Llandaff (S Glamorgan)
    Cathedral 81, 87
    St Michael's Theological College *87*
Lobb, Howard 25
Loddon (Norfolk)
    Housing 47
Loddon Rural District Council 12, 47
London
    A Imhof Ltd, New Oxford Street 103,
        112
    Ackroyden Estate 48, 49
    45–46 Albemarle Street 104, *120*
    Alexander Fleming House, Elephant
        & Castle 119
    Alton East Estate, Roehampton 12, 15,
        41–42, *48*, *49*, 50
    Alton West Estate, Roehampton 12,
        14, 20, 48, *50*, 51, 56, 71
    Bankside Power Station 110
    Bata, Oxford Street 103
    Battersea Power Station 46, 110
    Bousfield Primary School, South
        Kensington *16*, 21
    Bracken House, Cannon Street 20, 22
    Brandlehow Road Primary School,
        Wandsworth 36
    Britain Can Make It, Victoria & Albert
        Museum, 1946 18, 28
    Buzas residence, Ham 60
    Cafe Monico, Piccadilly Circus 22
    Castrol House, Marylebone Road 24,
        124
    Churchill Gardens, Pimlico 41, *46*, 49,
        71
    Housing, Claredale Street, Bethnal
        Green 21, 53
    Coronation decorations, 1953 10, 11, 18
    Croydon Airport 69
    1 Dean Trench Street 90
    10–12 Downing Street 22
    Primary school, Dulwich *31*
    Electricity Showroom, Regent Street 111
    Electrin House, 93–97 New Cavendish
        Street 104, *123*, *124*
    Fairlawn Primary School, Lewisham 61,
        102
    Ferranti exhibition stand, Radio Show,
        Earl's Court, 1952 117
    Festival of Britain 10–12, 15, 18,
        25–29, 80, 94, 95, 96, 102, 115,
        118
        Bailey Bridge, South Bank 29
        Dome of Discovery, South Bank 25,
            27
        Lion & Unicorn Pavilion, South Bank
            28
        Live Architecture Exhibition 84
        Pleasure Gardens, Battersea Park *93*
        Regatta Restaurant, South Bank 29
        Skylon, South Bank 27
        Telekinema, South Bank 18
        Thames-side Restaurant, South Bank
            28
    Finmar showrooms, Kingly Street *104*
    The Firs, Hampstead *19*, 21
    Gestetner flat, 12 Charles Street,
        Mayfair 66, 67

Golden Lane Estate, City of London
    11, 19, 21, 22, 41, *52*
Gooday residence, 36 West Temple
    Sheen 66
Great Exhibition, 1851 25
Hallfield School, Paddington 21
Housing, Ham Common, Richmond
    20, 42, *57*
Height restrictions 124
Highpoint I, Highgate 97
Housing, Holford Square 45
Holy Trinity, Dockhead 90
House of Commons 10
Hulton's Boys & Girls Exhibition,
    Olympia, 1956 117
Iceland Tourist Centre 111
Ideal Home Exhibitions 64, 65
    Canada Trend House, Ideal Home
        Exhibition, 1957 65
    House of the Future, Ideal Home
        Exhibition, 1956 19, *68*
    Kitchen for the Gas Council, Ideal
        Home Exhibition, 1955 64
Kidbrooke Comprehensive School,
    Corelli Road, Eltham *36*
Kon-Tiki Coffee Bar, St Mary Abbots
    Place 94, *95*
Lillington Gardens Estate, Pimlico 46
London (Heathrow) Airport 69, 76,
    77, 78
Mayfield Comprehensive School,
    Putney 17
Mermaid Theatre, Puddle Dock 94, *100*
Methodist Church, Cricket Green,
    Mitcham 89
Moro house, 20 Blackheath Park *61*
N M Rothschild offices, New Court 90
118–126 New Cavendish Street 123,
    124
New South Wales Government offices,
    Strand 114
Old Vic Theatre Annexe, The Cut 20,
    99
Our Lady of Mount Carmel,
    Kensington 81
Parkleys, Ham Common *54*
Paternoster Square, St Paul's 22
Peter Robinson Store, Strand *114*
Piazza Coffee Bar, Marylebone High
    Street, London 94, 95
Housing, Picton Street, Camberwell 17
The Priory, Blackheath 55
Housing, Priory Green 44, 45
Quantas, 69 Piccadilly 111
Royal Festival Hall, South Bank 2, 8,
    11, 14, 15, 17, 61, 96, 97, 98
St Paul's, Bow Common, Burdett Road
    91
St Paul's Cathedral 22
St Vedast's Rectory, City of London 22
Housing, Shacklewell Road 41
Shell garage, Kingston-upon-Thames 73
Shepherd's Bush Bus Garage 72
Housing, Somerford Grove, Hackney 41
South African Tourist Centre, 70
    Piccadilly 111
Six houses, South Hill Park, Hampstead
    20, *56*
Spa Green Estate, Rosebery Avenue 41,
    44, 45
Stockwell Bus Garage 72
Strand Comprehensive School 36
This Is Tomorrow exhibition,
    Whitechapel Art Gallery, 1956
    19, 94, *101*
Thorn House, Upper St Martin's Lane
    23, 24, 124
Thornton Heath Bus Garage 72
Time-Life International, New Bond
    Street, London 118
Tivoli Theatre, Strand 114
Torrington Furs, New Bond Street 103
Trades Union Congress, Great Russell
    Street *121*, *122*

Trinity Congregational Church, Poplar
    84, 89
Tulse Hill Comprehensive School 36
Housing, Usk Street, Bethnal Green
    21, 53
Vono Ltd, Grosvenor Street *113*
Wayang Coffee Lounge, Earl's Court
    Road 94
Westminster Abbey 22
Westville Road Primary School,
    Hammersmith 36, *102*
1–3 Willow Road, Hampstead 120
London County Council 36, 41, 102
    Architects Department 2, 6, 12, 13–14,
        15, 17, 20, *31*, 34, 36, *48*, *49*,
        50, *51*, 56, 61, 71, 75, 96, 97, 98
    Architects Department Photographic
        Unit 49, 51
    Housing Division 13–14, 15, 18, 48
London Transport 72
Lubetkin, Berthold 18, 44, 45 *See also*
    Skinner & Lubetkin; Skinner
    Bailey & Lubetkin; Tecton
Lucas, Colin 18, 50
Luton (Beds)
    St Luke, Leagrave 81
Lynch, Kevin 53
Lynn, Jack 51
Lyon, June 77
Lyons, Eric 21, *54*, *55*
Lyons Israel & Ellis 20, 99

McCallum, Ian 118
McCann, John 10, 43, 47, 64, 68, 77,
    80, 95, 98, 102, 113, 115
McHale, John *101*
Macmillan, Andy *85*
Macmillan, Harold 9, 41
McMorran, Donald 52
Maguire, Robert *85*, *91*
Maguire & Murray 83, *91*
Maltby, John 6, 11, 16, 26, 29, 33, 34,
    35, 36, 38, 44, 45, 46, 52, 64,
    65, 67, 73, 74, 76, 93, 94, 95,
    101, 107, 116, 117
Manasseh, Leonard 24
Manousso, Luke 57
Manousso, Paul 57
Marchwood (Hants)
    Marchwood Power Station *110*
Mardall, Cyril 18
Markelius, Sven 48
MARS Group 19, 25
Marseilles (France)
    Unité d'Habitation 20, 50, 53, 56
Martin, Sir J Leslie 2, 6, 14, 17, 61, 96, 97
Matthew, Sir Robert H 2, 6, 14, 69, *75*,
    96, 97
Maufe, Sir Edward 81
Meadows, Bernard 122
Medd, David 13, 30, 32, 33, *35*
Medd, Mary 15, 30, 32, *35*
Medley, Robert 86
Mellinger, Lucas 94
Metzstein, Isi *85*
Mies van der Rohe, Ludwig 18, 37, 104
Milan (Italy)
    Milan Triennale 1960 32
Miles, Bernard 100
Miller, John 99
Mills, Edward D 25, 81, 83, 88, *89*, 103
Miners' Welfare Architects Department
    108
Modular Society 16
Monktonhall (Midlothian)
    Colliery 108
Monsanto Chemicals 117
Montreal (Canada)
    World's Fair 1967 26
Moore, Henry *102*, 118
Moro, Peter 2, 6, 61, 94, 96, 97, 102
Morris & Steedman 21
Moscow (Russia)
    Centrosoyuz 121

INDEX 127

Motels 71
Mumford, Lewis 120

Naimski, Michael 94, *95*
Nairn, Ian 19, 22, 47
National Coal Board. Scottish Division 108
New Brutalism 18–21, 38, 78, 99
New Churches Research Group 83
New Empiricism 14–15, 48
New South Wales Government 114
New Towns 9, 12, 15–16, 26, 30, 43, 55
   Aycliffe (Durham) 15
   Corby (Northamptonshire) 15
   Crawley (W Sussex) 43, 116
   Cumbernauld (N Lanarkshire) 15
   Cwmbran (Torfaen) 15
   East Kilbride (S Lanarkshire) 15
   Glenrothes (Fife) 15, 85, 108
   Harlow (Essex) 15, 43
   Peterlee (Durham) 15, 18
   Stevenage (Herts) 11, 116
New York (NY)
   Lever House 24, 104, 123, 124
   Seagram Building 104
Newark (Notts)
   Barnby Road County Infants School *39*
Newbury (Berkshire)
   St John's 22
Newsom, John 30, 102
Nicholson, Ben 118
Nicholson, Sir Charles 81
Nigeria 18
Noble, C Wycliffe 66
Northfleet (Kent)
   Bowater 103
Nottingham (Notts)
   Playhouse Theatre 61, 94
Nottinghamshire County Architects Department 32, *39*
Nuttgens, Patrick 108

Ocean liners 74
Oddie, Guy 15
Office buildings 22, 24, 104, 118–124
Okeover Hall (Staffs) *63*
Orient Line 74
O'Rorke, E Brian 74
Osborn, Frederic 15
Osborne, John 98
Oswald, Arthur 63
Ove Arup & Partners *109*
Oxford (Oxon)
   Jaeger 113

Pace, George 81, *87*
Palladio, Andrea 62
Pantlin, John 31, 42, 46, 56, 70, 72, 84, *97*
Paolozzi, Sir Eduardo *101*
Paris (France)
   Maisons Jaoul 20, 21, 57
Parkin, P H 97
Partridge, John 50
Pasmore, Victor 29, 102
Pearl Assurance *118*
Percon 34
Perret, Auguste 120
Peterlee (Durham) 15, 18, 102
Pevsner, Sir Nikolaus 12, 18, 24, 40, 110
Philadelphia (Pa)
   Centennial Exposition, 1876 25
Philip Skelcher & Partners 103
Phillimore, Lord Claud 22, 63
Photographing architecture 38
Photomurals 113
Pick, Beverly 117
Picturesque 12, 15, 18, 26, 48, 49, 50, 58
Pile, W D 17
Piper, John 74
Piranesi, Giovanni Battista 45
Pitt, Peter 54, 55, 66
Pittsburgh (Pa)
   Alcoa Building 123

Plants, planting 29, 42, 66, 95, 111 *See also* Landscape & architecture
Plastics in building 68
Plastow, Norman F 94, *95*
Plymouth (Devon)
   Church of the Ascension, Crownhill 86
Poole (Dorset)
   Loewy Engineering 103
Pope, John Russell 63
Posener, Julius 44
Potter & Hare 86
Potters Bar (Herts)
   Potters Bar Railway Station *80*
Potts, David 118
Powell, Geoffrey 52
Powell & Moya 17, 21, *27*, 41, 43, *46*, 49, 71, 94
Power stations 110
Prefabrication, system building 9, 10, 13, 15, 17, 22, 24, 30, 32, 33, 35, 36, 37, 39, 42, 43, 73, 124
Price, Cedric 18

Quantas 111

R D Russell & Partners 74
Race, Ernest 29
Radburn (New Jersey) 71
Railways, railway stations 69, 78, 80
Reading (Berks)
   Shell-Mex & BP petrol station 73
Reid, D A 90
Reid, John & Sylvia 94, *95*
Richard Seifert & Partners 100
Richards, Sir James 15, 18, 20, 120
Richardson, Sir Albert 20, 22, 81
Riss, Egon *108*
Roads, road transport 69–73, 78, 116 *See also* Cars & traffic planning
Robert Matthew & Johnson-Marshall 21
Robert Matthew Johnson-Marshall & Partners 75
Robert Paine & Partners *70*
Rogers, Richard (Lord Rogers of Riverside) 13
Ronchamp (France)
   Notre-Dame-du-Haut 87
Rosenberg, Eugene 18
Rosenauer, Michael *118*
Rosenthal, H Werner 94
Rotterdam (Netherlands)
   Lijnbaan 116
Rowe, Colin 18
Rowntree, Diana 71
Rowntree, Kenneth 102
Royal Institute of British Architects 17, 18, 94, 107
   Architectural Science Group 16
Russell, R D *28*, 118 *See also* R D Russell & Partners

Saint, Andrew 33
St Leonards-on-Sea (E Sussex)
   St John the Evangelist 90
Sanderson, Joseph 63
Scarfe, Laurence 29, 74
Scharoun, Hans 121
Schinkel, Karl Friedrich 22
Schools 12–13, 22, 30–39, 102
Scott, Sir Giles Gilbert 10, 18, 81, 110
Sculpture *See* Art in relation to architecture
Seely & Paget 81
Segal, Walter 18
Seifert, Richard 22, 24 *See also* Richard Seifert & Partners
Shaw, Richard Norman 90
Sheffield (S Yorks)
   Park Hill 51
   St Paul's, Wordsworth Avenue, Ecclesfield *88*
   Arts block, Sheffield University 40
   Library, Sheffield University *40*
Shell-Mex & BP 73

Shepherd, Maria 29
Shopping centres 103, 115, 116
Shops, showrooms 103, 111–114
   shop fronts 103–104, 111, 112, 113
Sir William Halcrow & Partners *110*
Sisson, Marshall 63
Skidmore Owings & Merrill 24, 104, 123, 124
Skinner & Lubetkin 44, 45
Skinner Bailey & Lubetkin 45
Slater Uren & Pike 36
Smith, Ivor 51
Smithson, Alison & Peter 18–19, *37*, 38, 47, *68*, 81, *101*, 107
Smithson, Peter 38
Snoek, Henk 23, *40*, 82, 88, 89, 114, 124
Soane, Sir John 62
Span Developments Ltd 21, 42, 54, 55
Spence, Sir Basil 18, *23*, 24, 81, *82*, 83, *88*, 94, 124
Squire, Raglan 10
SS Oriana 74
Stark, D Rogers *84*, 89
Steel construction 13, 33, 37, 38, 39, 73, 76, 78, 107, 112
Stevenage (Herts) 11
   Barclay School *102*
   Sish Lane 43
   Town centre 71, *116*
Stillman, C G 12
Stirling, Sir James 18, 24, 57, 94, 99
Stirling & Gowan 9, 20, 42, *57*
Stjernstedt, Rosemary 48
Stockholm (Sweden)
   Exhibition of Modern Industrial & Decorative Arts, 1930 14, 25
Stonework 58, 62, 66, 86, 87, 111
Summerson, Sir John 17, 22, 69, 94
Sutton, Carl 117
Swain, E E 37
Swain, Henry 33, 39
Swedish influence on design 10–11, 14–15, 20, 21, 24, 25, 33, 48, 50, 66, 69, 84

Tayler, Herbert 103–104, 112
Tayler & Green 9, 12, *14*, 21, 47, 103, *112*
Team working, group working 12–13, 14, 17, 30, 32, 37, 96, 105, 109
Team X 19
Tecton 41, *44*, *45*, 97
Television 9, 92, 98, 100
Tempest, H 105
Terry, Quinlan 62
Theatres 94, 99, 100
   open stage 94, 100
Thomas, Mark Hartland 16
Thompson, Paul 53
Thornton (Fife)
   Rothes Colliery *108*
Tiles, tilework 79, 80
Timber, use of 21, 28, 58, 61, 65, 66, 75, 111
Time-Life International *118*
Tinling, Teddy 68
Toomey, W J 75, 85
Town & Country Planning Association 15
Townsend, Geoffrey 54
Trades Union Congress *121*, *122*
Traffic in Towns 71
Travers, Stanley 87
Tubbs, Ralph 25, *27*
Tunnard, John 29, 61

US influence on design 15, 24, 60, 101, 104, 118, 123, 124
Universities, university campuses 11, 24, 30, 40

Vällingby (Sweden) 48
Vanbrugh, Sir John 20
Venice (Italy)
   Santa Fosca, Torcello 91

Ventris, Michael 35
Vernacular architecture, structures 15, 20, 57
Vézelay, Paule 101
Victorian Society 22
Vincent, Leonard G 116
Voelcker, John *101*
Vono Ltd *113*

W E Middleton & Son Ltd 39
Waleran Committee 73
Wales & Monmouthshire Industrial Estates Ltd 105
Ward, Basil 18
Ward, Neville 117
Ward & Austin 74
Warsaw (Poland) 115
Watson, James Fletcher 81
Watt, Elizabeth 62
Welwyn Garden City (Herts)
   8 Ashley Close *42*
Westminster City Council 46
Westwood, Bryan 112
Westwood, Colin *2*, *27*, 28, 29, 33, 57, 76, 78, 79, 86, 96, 98, 100, 102, 109, 120, 121, 122, 123
Westwood, Norman 112
Whitehead, David 66
Williams, Alan 20
Williams, Edwin *2*, 6, 96, *97*
Williams, Sir E Owen 103
Wilson, Angus 83
Wilson, Colin St John 18
Wilson, Hugh 15
Wilson, Josephine 100
Windows, glazing 34, 37, 38, 66, 74, 86, 87, 88, 98, 109, 111, 113, 114, 119, 123, 124
   picture windows 42, 59, 60, 103–104
Windsor (Berks)
   Isokon Estate, St Leonard's Hill 50
Witham (Essex)
   Cooper Taber & Co, Station Road *107*, 109
Wittkower, Rudolf 18, 91
Wokingham (Berks)
   St Crispin's Secondary Modern School 32, *35*
Woman 65
Womersley, J L 51
Womersley, Peter 21, *58*, *59*
Wren, Sir Christopher 81
Wright, Frank Lloyd 58

Yardleys 113
Yates, Peter 45
Yorke, F R S 18
Yorke Rosenberg & Mardall 17, 18, 21, 43, 69, 71, *78*, 79, *102*
Yugoslavia 98

(page references in italic indicate illustrations)